PENGUIN BOOKS

THE WAR LOR]

A J P Taylor was born at Birkdale in Lancashire in 1906. He was educated at Bootham School, York, and at Oriel College, Oxford. He was a lecturer in Modern History at Manchester University from 1930 to 1938, and from then until 1976 a Fellow of Magdalen College, Oxford, of which he then became an Honorary Fellow. He was an Honorary Fellow of Oriel College, Oxford, and a Fellow of the British Academy. He was Ford's Lecturer in English History at Oxford from 1955 to 1956 and Leslie Stephen Lecturer at Cambridge from 1960 to 1961. During 1976 he was Joseph Meaker Visiting Professor at Bristol University, and gave the Creighton Lecture at London University and the Andrew Lang Lecture at St Andrews. A J P Taylor was an honorary D.C.L. of the University of New Brunswick, D.Univ. of York University and honorary D.Litt of Bristol, Warwick and Manchester Universities. He was an honorary member of the American Academy of Arts and Sciences and of the Hungarian Academy of Sciences.

He gave many history lectures on television and was the only lecturer to face the camera for half an hour without notes or visual aids. He contributed regularly to the *Observer* and *The London Review of Books*.

His books include *The Course of German History*, *The Struggle for Mastery in Europe, 1848–1918*, *Bismarck*, *From Sarajevo to Potsdam*, *My Darling Pussy: the Correspondence of Lloyd George and Frances Stevenson*, *The Last of Old Europe*, *The Russian War 1941–1945*, *How Wars Begin*, *A Personal History*, his autobiography, *How Wars End* and *An Old Man's Diary*. A number of his books have been published in Penguin: *The Origins of the Second World War*, *The Habsburg Monarchy*, *The First World War: an Illustrated History*, *English History 1914–1945*, *Beaverbrook*, *The Second World War: an illustrated History*, *Essays in English History*, and *The Trouble Makers*. He also contributed a long introduction to the Penguin edition of *The Communist Manifesto*.

A J P Taylor died in September 1990. In his obituary, *The Times* paid tribute to him as 'Probably the most controversial, and certainly the best known, historian in the English-speaking world. In his prime A J P Taylor attracted – and usually bewitched – a wider following than Macaulay ever dreamt of. Prolific and best-selling author, gifted journalist, and *sui generis* as a television star, he attempted to transform the historical understanding of his day', while the *Independent* described him as 'The best-known historian of his generation ... a technically outstanding historian, with two special qualities: intuition – what he himself called his 'green fingers' – and a unique gift for making ordinary language carry extraordinary thought'.

A J P Taylor

# THE WAR LORDS

PENGUIN BOOKS

PENGUIN BOOKS

Published by the Penguin Group
Penguin Books Ltd, 27 Wrights Lane, London W8 5TZ, England
Penguin Books USA Inc., 375 Hudson Street, New York, New York 10014, USA
Penguin Books Australia Ltd, Ringwood, Victoria, Australia
Penguin Books Canada Ltd, 10 Alcorn Avenue, Toronto, Ontario, Canada M4V 3B2
Penguin Books (NZ) Ltd, 182–190 Wairau Road, Auckland 10, New Zealand

Penguin Books Ltd, Registered Offices: Harmondsworth, Middlesex, England

First published in Great Britain by Hamish Hamilton 1977
Published in Penguin Books 1978
9 10

Printed in England by Clays Ltd, St Ives plc

# Contents

# Illustrations

## STALIN

# *Preface*

This book contains the transcripts of six lectures which I delivered on BBC television in August 1976. I gave the lectures in my usual fashion without script or illustrations, simply talking to camera and making things up as I went along. I have tidied up the text for publication, removing occasional muddles or false starts. Otherwise the lectures appear exactly as I delivered them.

Five of the lectures are biographical studies of the men who exercised supreme power during the Second World War; the sixth explains why there was no such man in Japan nor indeed any supreme direction at all. There is a deeper theme. Most wars in modern times have been run by a confusion of committees and rival authorities. The Second World War was uniquely different. In September 1939 the British and French governments declared war on Germany. Otherwise virtually every great decision of the Second World War was made by one of these five men except when the chaotic anarchy of Japan intervened. Each of the five was unmistakably a war lord, determining the fate of mankind. Yet each had an individual character and method that makes generalisation difficult.

Three were avowedly dictators; two exercised their dictatorship with an outward respect for constitutional forms. One, Mussolini, was lazy. Three ran the operations of war from day to day, Stalin almost from hour to hour. Roosevelt observed the war with casual detachment until the moment for decision arrived. All had served in the First World War, though Roosevelt served only in a civilian office. Four were prolific writers; Roosevelt never wrote anything, not even his own speeches. Four were masters of the radio; only Stalin owed his power entirely to other means. Two were amateur painters; one was an amateur violinist. One was the grandson of a duke. One came from a rich professional family. One was the son of a customs official. Two were the sons of humble workers. Only one received a university education. One was happily married. One ran after every woman who came in sight. One was unhappily married. One was a widower. The fifth married only the day before he died.

This was a bewildering variety. But the five had some things in common. Each of them dominated the service chiefs. Each determined his policy of his country. All five were set on victory, though of course not all could achieve it. They provided the springs of action throughout the years of war. This was an astonishing assertion of the Individual in what is often known as the age of the masses.

# 1

# MUSSOLINI

# Mussolini

'War lord' is a word rather like our currency—it is much depreciated. Nowadays, we use 'war lord' about almost any general or almost any political leader who rules in a dictatorial way. The true war lord was a man of great, of unique, power, dominating both the military and civil affairs of his country; a dictator whose power was unlimited and who made all the vital decisions. Attila the Hun was a war lord of a primitive kind; Napoleon was a war lord.

In the First World War, curiously enough, there were no war lords. Lloyd George liked to call himself the man who won the war, but he did so despite great opposition from the generals and he was very rarely able to get his own way. Even the German generals Hindenburg and Ludendorff, though often called war lords, operated within fairly strict limits.

The Second World War, on the other hand, though we like to call it, and rightly to call it, the People's War, was also the war of the war lords. Of the six great powers involved in the Second World War, all except one had a single acknowledged leader from whom all the basic decisions and forces sprang. The first of the modern dictators, though by no means the most successful, was Benito Mussolini, leader, Duce, of Italy.

Mussolini operated altogether for some 20 years and introduced the modern conception of dictatorship, a dictatorship which claimed to spring from the people, not to be imposed from above by a monarch.

*Mussolini, 1910, the Socialist*

Mussolini was very much a man of the people himself. His father was a blacksmith; he, when young, was a revolutionary socialist. If Bolshevik had been in the early 20th century a term that applied outside Russia, Mussolini would have been called a Bolshevik. But during the First World War he broke with his socialist comrades and, though still calling himself a man of the left, championed the war.

It is worth asking of each of these war lords—what did he know of war? Mussolini served in the trenches—and the Italian trenches were perhaps the worst trenches in Europe, with the harshest conditions, where nothing was done for the ordinary men. He served in the trenches for two years; he was then invalided out because of a wound and came back into politics at the end of the war.

It was then that he broke with his socialist comrades. He organised a group of ex-servicemen; a Fascist party was the party he invented. Fascism merely means an organised group of people. The significant thing about what Mussolini did was that he transformed this group of ex-servicemen into a group used as strike-

*Mussolini, 1917, the soldier*

breakers, attacking the co-operatives, attacking the trade unions, co-operating with the employers to resist the revolutionary working-class movement.

By 1922, Mussolini had built up an aggressive political party, and he threatened, somewhat grandiloquently, that the forces of this Fascist party—who wore black shirts, where the name 'Black Shirts' came from—would march on Rome. There was a great deal more talk of marching and the Italian crowds surging around in their own towns than there was a real march. When there was so much disturbance, the king succumbed. The army said they did not want to be used in civil disputes; the king said: 'The only alternative, then, is to make Mussolini prime minister.' Mussolini was summoned to Rome; he didn't march there—he went by train overnight. He stepped, black-shirted, into his sleeping-car and emerged at Rome in a top hat and frock-coat. He had been transformed into the respectable prime minister of Italy.

And indeed during the first two or three years he was by no means a dictator. He was playing the game of parliament, building up coalitions. It was only gradually that he used the illegal force of the Fascist party—the beating-up of opponents, the beginnings in a cautious way of a reign of terror—and so arrived at a dictatorial position. The final thing which carried him to dictatorship was the murder of one of his most courageous opponents, Matteotti, a socialist. This murder shook the prestige of the régime. Mussolini himself lost his nerve. And then, because his opponents were ineffective, he resumed, and established the single-party state which existed from 1925 until his fall in 1943.

He himself, as well as prime minister, acquired the official title of leader, Duce, the first time that such a title had been used, except in purely military terms. And this was his justification for claiming supreme power. When you consider Italian policy

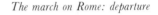

*The march on Rome: departure*

*The march on Rome: arrival*

thereafter, from 1925, it all turned on Mussolini. But it turned in a rather casual way. When it came to government, he was a lazy man. I have turned over pages of the foreign office documents which were sent to Mussolini—he sat there with the vast desk almost empty of papers, because all he did was to write at the end of every two or three that he picked up the word *importante*. It was the only comment he ever made, so he can't have had to work frightfully hard in judging foreign affairs. What he did was to create an impression of power. Just as he had bluffed himself into political power, so he bluffed Italy, and himself as Duce of Italy, into the position of being a great power.

He was the only European ruler of the 1920s who talked openly in terms of great military power. When other countries were pursuing, or alleged that they were pursuing, disarmament, Italy was launching a new, great, rearmament programme. All the political demonstrations in Mussolini's Italy were of an apparently military kind. He was one of the first modern politicians to use the cinema as a political weapon. Marches of apparently highly disciplined troops or young people, demonstrations of Italian might in the air, demonstrations of the great Italian navy. Most of these things were, in fact, demonstrations and not much else. Italy was, after all, a poor country, and the actual expenditure on rearmament had to be restricted all the time. Mussolini believed that show would carry the day.

I think one can say a bit more than that. He was deluded and led astray himself by the shows that he put on. As he looked at these masses of marching troops shown to him on the screen, he really believed that Italy had an army of five million. The actual figure was not much more than a million when it came to the point. The five million was a phrase he had once used; he used it so often, it got into his own head. In exactly the same way, he came to believe that Italy had the most powerful navy in the Mediterranean.

At the same time, he played his role as a European statesman. He was accepted by others. Sir Austen Chamberlain not only sent

*Matteotti, the murdered Socialist*

*Mussolini takes a jump*

*European Statesmen:*
*Mussolini and Austen*
*Chamberlain*

*Mussolini at the Pontine Marshes*

him Christmas cards, but actually joined him on holiday with his family. This aristocratic Englishman and Mussolini, the son of a blacksmith, exchanged greetings and treated each other as equals. Mussolini came to enjoy a unique position of respect in Europe. The very stability of his régime, or so it appeared—it is not difficult to have a stable régime if you put all your opponents in prison, and threaten to beat up others who cause trouble—the very stability of his régime, the fact that he had been in power so long, led people to think that he had become a senior statesman, a man of great wisdom, always consulted.

The new phase of Mussolini's life came with the rise of a second Fascist dictator, Hitler, a man of very different character, much stronger, and with much greater resources behind him. This is a curious thing: Mussolini, with such few resources, was yet the one man whom Hitler genuinely accepted as an equal. And the only one whom Hitler genuinely took seriously. The conferences which they held together, though they look now to us so comical, were demonstrations—at any rate on Hitler's side—of great power. And Mussolini himself was dragged forward into becoming more assertive, more aggressive, simply because of the challenge from his fellow dictator.

Mussolini always displayed the physical attributes of dictatorship. He was, although not tall, extremely powerful, and, in the intervals of displaying his troops, he would display himself as

*Mussolini goes to War*

*Mussolini and the King of Italy*

*The two dictators in Rome*

a powerful rider, horsejumper. He would also love showing off his physical prowess. When the unemployed had been set to work clearing the Pontine Marshes, Mussolini often turned up, stripped to the waist, and would then join them, digging away, showing that he was tough and strong as he had been when he was a blacksmith's son.

Mussolini was one of the first who fully appreciated the danger from a reviving Germany; and at one time he was associated with Great Britain and France in some sort of plan by which they hoped to check Germany. Two things pulled Mussolini the other way, and this was, indeed, where his decisions affected the fate of Italy throughout the Second World War, and for many years thereafter. His first decision was that, in order to increase Italian power, he launched a war in Abyssinia, and conquered Abyssinia in a very short time. Although he himself had little to do with the plans, his was the final decision both to make the war and, when it was on, to press it on more urgently. His general in command hesitated and said: 'It will take two years.' Mussolini said: 'We

can't wait that long, you must finish it this season.' And he suc-
ceeded, so that his first great military order was vindicated by
success.

The second decision he made was of a far graver nature. If he
adhered to the allied side of Great Britain and France, Italy
would be in the front line—and would be overwhelmed by German power before Great Britain and France could do anything to
help her. If, on the other hand, he associated himself with Hitler,
then he would be carried to success: his own bluff would not be
exposed. In 1936, he established the confidential relations with
Hitlerite Germany which he called the Axis, on which Europe
was then supposed to revolve. And, from that time on,
Mussolini—despite his constant alarms, despite the apprehensions that Italy would not be able to carry her weight, would not
remain a great power when faced with the challenge of war—

*The two dictators in the field*

Mussolini was tied to Hitler's side.

His last great moment, I suppose, was the conference at Munich in 1938. It was he who proposed it; he appeared as the supremely great, independent statesman, negotiating between Germany on the one hand, Great Britain and France on the other. The actual Munich Agreement is what Mussolini pulled out of his bag—he was given it by the Germans first, but he didn't reveal this. He, as the impartial arbitrator, said: 'This is the deal

*The meeting at Munich, 1938*

*Neville Chamberlain and Lord Halifax in Rome*

that we should make'; and the others accepted. For a little time, he enjoyed the fame of a peacemaker, a fame as undeserved as any of the others.

In September 1939, war broke out between Germany on the one side and Britain and France on the other. Mussolini evaded the challenge. He explained to Hitler that, while he was entirely on Germany's side, Italy was not ready. He said: 'We need another three years.' And Hitler, who saw more clearly that Italy was no great asset, accepted this. Nine months later, when France fell, Mussolini was afraid that he was going to be left out of the war. The decision was entirely his own; the king was against war, the generals were against war; Ciano, the foreign minister, was against war. Mussolini thought: 'Unless I go to war now before France collapses. I shall have missed the boat.' Later on, he complained that it was all the others who were for war, and he said, somewhat cynically: 'I was the only pacifist.' I think he was exaggerating.

Italy went to war under Mussolini in the belief that when the war was over, she would come out with large prizes and no effort. Instead, although the French collapsed, Great Britain continued,

*At the opera*

and won the Battle of Britain. And with Germany secure for the time being in Europe, all the weight of British pressure fell on Italy.

From August 1940 until mid-1943, the war, so far as Britain was concerned, was mainly a war against Italy, not against Germany, and it was a war which Italy could not sustain. Mussolini accumulated mistakes—again, they were all his. Without doubt, his was the idea of an offensive campaign in North Africa which, within a few months, brought the Italian army to disaster. Even more alarming was his decision, having annexed Albania, to invade Greece. He did this for a very characteristic reason—he said he was tired of getting messages every day from Hitler saying: 'I've started a war with somebody.' He said: 'This time, I'll be able to send a message to Hitler saying I've started a war with somebody; I've invaded Greece.' This was an exaggeration because, as soon as the Italians advanced from Albania, the Greeks pushed them back. Hitler was later to claim that Mussolini's declaration of war against Greece lost him the war, because with the increasing disasters of the Italian forces in Greece, the Germans had to go to the assistance of the Italians, and thus postpone the invasion of Russia.

This is a somewhat speculative view; it is an excuse which Hitler gave thereafter. The best view nowadays—which is mine, I may say, as well as that of other people, or, shall I say, other people's as well as mine—is that the German assistance in Greece which led to the complete conquest of Greece and of Yugoslavia too did not in fact have any decisive effect on delaying the Ger-

*Mussolini sends troops to Albania*

*Italian troops disembarking at Durazzo*

man invasion of Russia.

From this moment, Italy had lost the war. She was kept in the war only by German support, by German troops, first of all in Greece, and then, increasingly, by German troops in North Africa, by Rommel and the Afrika Korps. By the end of 1942, it was quite clear that North Africa was going to be lost, and that Italy, from every point of view—from the naval point of view, from the military point of view—was a defeated power.

In the early months of 1943, the only question was: would the Allies invade Italy? They did so—they landed in Sicily. Inside Italy, the only practical question was: how could Italy get out of the war? Mussolini himself admitted that she must do so. Ostensibly, he was commander-in-chief, a position he had given himself at the beginning of the war in 1940. In fact, he had completely lost control of the war. He told his closest associates that he was going to tell Hitler the war was over; Italy must get out. But when he had his last meeting as Duce, with Hitler, at Feltre, he couldn't bring himself to say it; and, when he came back to Rome, he said the war must go on.

There was a series of conspiracies. Some generals said they

*Italian artillery stuck in the snow*

*Hands up*

*Italian prisoners at Tobruk*

would get rid of Mussolini; some politicians said they would get rid of Mussolini; the king said he would get rid of Mussolini; none of them did so. In the end, curiously enough, Mussolini got rid of himself. In the Grand Council, as it was called, the Fascists met; the great majority expressed a lack of confidence in Mussolini. Mussolini said angrily: 'You have provoked the crisis of the régime.' But he didn't indicate he was going to take their advice.

The next day he went to the king and said: 'The Grand Council has lost confidence in me; I resign as commander-in-chief —someone else can carry on the war.' He thought he would stay as Duce, but the king had already prepared a coup d'état. Mussolini was stopped by police as he left the palace, put into an ambulance so that no one would notice, and exiled to an island.

Fascism collapsed overnight; not a single Fascist attempted to defend the régime which had lasted 20 years, and had boasted itself of such power. It simply fell down like a house of cards, which was all it really was. The Italian rulers, however, were afraid that Mussolini might be grabbed by raiders on the island.

*The road to Mersa Matruh*

*Italian prisoners leaving Tobruk*

They moved him to a mountain. There, they thought, at the top of a mountain in a sort of health resort, he would be secure. But, by a daring operation, German paratroops landed on the mountain, and rescued Mussolini and took him to Munich. You can see a newsreel of him arriving—an absolutely broken, shattered man. He said all he wanted to do was to go to his country home and spend his time in retirement at Rocca delle Caminate. Hitler would not allow it. 'Once a dictator,' he said, 'always a dictator.' He insisted that Mussolini should go back, and there was then a sort of shadow, an imitation, of Fascism set up in northern Italy, on Lake Garda, at a place called Salo—so it's called the republic of Salo. Mussolini once more claimed to be Duce. 'The Italian Social Republic,' he said, 'should this time be really a republic of the left.' He went back to his old left-wing ideas. 'Ah,' he said, 'what a mistake I made in allowing the king and the aristocracy and the capitalists to survive. I thought I could control them. I ought to have rubbed them out, and ruled in the name of the workers.'

*British troops land in Sicily*

He had a council of ministers; the Italian minister of war was even allowed to raise a few troops. In fact, Mussolini's power did not extend outside the wretched hall where the council of ministers met. Lake Garda was up in the mountains; it rained most of the time, and Mussolini used to stare out through the rain and say: 'We're all dead.' He wasn't allowed to move without a German controller. Parts of Italy—South Tyrol, Trieste—were transferred from Italian to German control. He saw that, far from gaining, he was losing territory for Italy. The Italian army had no real existence. Some of the troops acted as auxiliaries to the Germans—most were not allowed to act at all. The only thing that Mussolini was compelled to do was to put on trial those Fascists who had expressed lack of confidence in him, and have them all sentenced to death, among them his own son-in-law Ciano. And he did not resist. The life had gone out of him.

He had one last moment of grandeur. On 20 July 1944, there was a bomb attempt on Hitler's life. Hitler was a shattered man. Here again, you can see this in a newsreel—Hitler's left arm completely paralysed. And, exactly at that moment, Mussolini arrived on a visit. He stepped out of the train, shambling and inferior, and, at last, saw Hitler down and himself up. And one of the most delightful touches in any war film is to see Mussolini swelling up, patting Hitler on the shoulders and saying: 'Well, it isn't so bad after all; I'll stand by you.' That was the last meeting in grandeur of the two dictators.

At the beginning of 1945, strangely enough, Mussolini was still enormously popular. He had great meetings in Milan, but as the Allies advanced, and as the Italian partisans rose, Mussolini knew that everything was lost. At the last minute, he tried to negotiate with the partisans to surrender; he even talked as though he himself had always been anti-German, and should be welcomed as the first of the partisans. He got no welcome from them, and at that moment he learned that the German forces were withdrawing from Milan. He felt that they were betraying him.

By then, it is fair to say, he had lost any sense of reality. Where, if he tried to escape, was he to escape to? He was simply on the move. He left Salo because he thought he could discuss matters with somebody in Milan. Now, although he had met the partisan leaders, they had nothing to offer him. Indeed, they had warned him that he was regarded as the public enemy. At the last minute,

*The hotel on Gran Sasso*

38

*Mussolini and his rescuers at Gran Sasso*

he joined a German convoy of trucks and tanks which was setting off through the Alps back to Germany.

In the narrow roads along Lake Como, they were held up by a partisan barrier. The German tanks could have shot their way through, but they didn't want any more trouble, they wanted to go home. And the Italians said: 'All right, we'll let you go through on condition you're not taking any Italians with you.' As they searched the trucks, they found a man in a German greatcoat; they pulled him out—it was Mussolini. There were other Italian ministers who were also caught on the same convoy; they were pulled out. The partisans had no doubt at all what to do with the ministers—they took them down to the nearest town and shot them that evening.

Mussolini was too big a fish for them. So they concealed him in a farm building well off the road. By a—I was going to say a strange chance, but it's not correct—by deliberation, Mussolini was joined by his mistress, Clara Petacci. Before this time, Mussolini had said farewell to his family, told them it was all over—he had tried to do his best for Italy, but they should not come with

39

*Mussolini and his liberator*

*Clara Petacci, the faithful mistress*

him. Clara Petacci, who had been his mistress for a very long time—not the only mistress Mussolini had had by any means—pursued him, joined up with him, and was also interned in the farmhouse.

Next morning, a partisan communist leader, who was driving up the valley, heard that there was some significantly great Fascist hidden up in the mountains. He had armed himself with a warrant, somewhat speculatively perhaps, entitling him to deal with Mussolini as he saw best. He and a friend drove their lorry up to the farmhouse; Mussolini and Clara Petacci, because there was nowhere else for them to be, were in bed. They got out. Mussolini believed he was being rescued and said to the communist leader: 'You have come to rescue me, I will give you an empire.' The last of his illusions or pretences. Clara Petacci, being practical-minded, was fumbling under the bedclothes. The par-

*Mussolini's last public appearance, Milan*

*The end for Mussolini and Clara Petacci*

tisan thought she was looking for a gun, and said: 'What are you doing?' She said: 'I'm looking for my knickers.' They were taken out to a nearby quarry. Mussolini was stood against the wall. When Clara saw that they were going to shoot him, she stood in front of him. They were both shot dead. Their bodies were left there for some hours, and then taken down to Milan. The violence displayed against their bodies was so great that, to put them out of reach, they were hung upside down outside a garage. A picture that can be often seen, which signifies, in a sense, Mussolini's end. Poor Mussolini, as someone said, always upside down, a man doomed to failure.

After a day or two, somebody managed to rescue the body, and it was taken away and hidden for some years in a monastery. The treasures which Mussolini carried with him were never found, if indeed they existed. Some years later, Mussolini's body was quietly moved to a family grave where it now obscurely rests.

# 2
# HITLER

# Hitler

Adolf Hitler, German Chancellor, Führer or leader of the German people, made all on his own the decision which transformed a limited war in Europe into a great war. And he made a second decision, again on his own, which transformed that great European war into the Second World War. Adolf Hitler was many things. People have debated his philosophies, his geopolitics, his racialism, but, in my opinion, he was essentially, fundamentally, a war lord.

In the First World War, he had risen only to the rank of lance-corporal, but he was a very devoted soldier, acquiring the Iron Cross, first class—a rare distinction for an ordinary soldier—and was shattered by Germany's defeat in 1918. Everything sprang from that. What Hitler wanted to do was to bring Germany back to being a great power; to undo all the effects of Germany's defeat and then continue on from a victorious Germany to make Germany the great power of Europe.

He used many methods for this, including political agitation; in 1923, indeed, he tried a political revolt, which failed, but he learned from it how to proceed to pervert the constitutional process. He built up a great party, the National Socialist Party, which had a constructive programme of a sort. He exploited the Great Depression, and it was, indeed, the mass unemployment in Germany which carried him to power.

But from that time, from the moment he became chancellor, his thoughts were on the recovery of Germany. There are those

*Hitler the front line soldier*

who say that he wanted a great war. I would rather say that he wanted a great victory. Whether this would be achieved by war or by overwhelming moral pressure—or immoral pressure—I think was unimportant to him.

Curiously enough, he was, not only in political matters but in military matters, a great propagandist. He always exaggerated very greatly the military preparations that he made. In 1936, for instance, the best guesses of British Intelligence were about 100 per cent too great. In 1940, when the German army was supposed to have been overwhelming and to have defeated the French by a mass of metal, the French in fact had more tanks than the Germans. And by 1940, Great Britain was producing more tanks, more aeroplanes—in fact, more of everything except rifles—than Germany, and kept ahead all through the war. It was not so much that Germany had more armaments, but that from quite an early stage, Hitler said she had.

If you look at the record before the war, as he was moving, as it were, more towards a warlike situation, he achieved his successes by overawing the other side. The Munich conference, the settle-

*Hitler the agitator*

ment of 1938, is the supreme example of this.

Most of the evidence indicates that Hitler contemplated war in 1938 only when he realised that the other side, the British and French, had already given in. And I think we can go further, though I must say that other historians have disputed this. Even in 1939, when Germany went to war with Poland, this was, perhaps, not a mistake or miscalculation. The Polish war lasted for three weeks at most. The German casualties were very light; it was a war that was over almost before it had begun. And Hitler seems to have assumed that the British and French—who had done nothing to help Poland, could not do anything to help her—would fold up.

Up to this time, Hitler's direction of military affairs had been remote. He was, as chancellor, and later as Hindenburg's successor as president, theoretically the supreme commander, but of course the command was, in fact, exercised by professionals, generals, very few of whom regarded Hitler with sincere loyalty. There was, until 1938, a war minister, who took all the great strategical decisions. In 1938, Hitler had a stroke of luck. The war minister married a woman who had a record as a prostitute—or really, I suspect, just as a nude model. At any rate, he was discredited and driven to resign. No new war minister was appointed. So from that moment, Hitler was the practical head of the three services.

He never attempted to combine them. He always operated with each separately, kept them distinct, in a sense, in rivalry—army, navy, air force. There was still a commander-in-chief of the army, as of the air force and navy, who actually carried out the operations. It was the commander-in-chief, Rundstedt, who, in Poland, decided things. It was the supreme commander-in-chief, Brauchitsch, who was responsible for the overall direction.

When, in the autumn of 1939, Hitler insisted that France was not going to make peace and there must be an offensive, the generals hesitated. And at one of the meetings—a dramatic moment—Hitler pointed, not to the outskirts, to the Belgian

*Hitler the political leader*

coast, which was where the generals were thinking of advancing, but to the centre, and said: 'Why can't I go through there?' This was the origin of the most brilliant strategic stroke of the Second World War: the strategic stroke which, in May 1940, disrupted entirely the French front, produced not only a defeat but a castastrophe for the French army, which within a few weeks had collapsed, and with virtually no loss to the German forces. Germany achieved not only the defeat of France, but supremacy over Europe, with some 25,000 dead—about as many as the British army, in the First World War, lost on the Somme in a single day. And it was, though carried out by others, Hitler's stroke of genius which did it.

It is said he made a mistake in allowing the British Expedi-

*Hitler leaving a meeting*

*Hitler and Hindenburg*

tionary Force to escape at Dunkirk. There was, I think, a good deal of confusion. It was not a brilliant inspiration, certainly. On the other hand, the general in command there, Rundstedt, also hesitated. Goering said he could destroy the BEF from the air, and, in any case, it never crossed Hitler's mind that Great Britain would continue the war once France had been defeated.

The Battle of Britain was not an inspiration of his. He took no interest in it—it is the only one of his campaigns which he never attended. He went off to Berchtesgaden, because I think he suspected from the beginning that there would be no invasion.

But thereafter began the development of his power. For one thing, he had proved all the German generals wrong. They had all said a total defeat of France was impossible. They had worked out their details in their old-fashioned way, and this man, who had no experience of war except as a corporal, who had not particularly studied the great military writings of the past, by a single stroke of inspiration had achieved this staggering victory.

It is often said—and it became true later on in the Second World War—that the victor in an offensive needed a five-to-one supremacy if he were going to carry it through. The Germans, in 1940, had no such supremacy at all. They were about level with the French, and yet they destroyed what, until that time, had been regarded as the greatest army in Europe.

From June 1940 until June 1941, except for air attacks and a minor conflict in Greece, there was peace on the continent of Europe. Hitler had achieved what no previous great man, not even Napoleon, had achieved: he had brought all Europe up to the Russian frontier under his domination. Some of the countries had been conquered; some, though not many, of the territories had been annexed to Germany. Some of them had become satellites reluctantly; some of them had become satellites more willingly and were co-operating. Two, Switzerland and Sweden, were technically independent, but, because of their geographical position, were bound to the German economic war-machine.

*Hitler and his Japanese allies*

*Hitler as Dictator*

Now Hitler could really look over the whole of Europe and envisage it all being operated for the increasing strength and power of Germany. Germany had certainly become a great power. And there are those who speculate why he did not stop, as, for instance, Bismarck had known how to stop.

One answer, I suppose, is quite simple: if you are a war lord, you do not like giving up. Hitler used other arguments. One was simply that, with a great army in existence—and he did not want to demobilise it until he had completed his campaigns—he must do something. English people, who think in maritime terms, in terms of the navy and overseas operations, express surprise that Hitler never tried to invade North Africa through Spain—or even, for that matter, tried to invade the Middle East through Turkey. I think, basically, these were psychologically without appeal to Hitler, because they did not demand the operation of great land-power. He was very much the man of the continent. Also, he was a man, despite his victories, full of apprehensions.

By 1941, he was absolutely convinced that, unless he struck a blow against Russia first and knocked the Russians out, they would, one day, when perhaps his conflict with Britain had got more acute, turn against him; they would betray him. He sometimes pleaded that he needed to dominate the resources of Russia, but, ironically, these were pouring into Germany until the very day that the Germans invaded Russia. One consequence of Hitler's invasion was that the supplies were cut off.

At any rate—and this is the point with which I began—all Hitler's earlier decisions had been, in part, responses to others. The Polish campaign was a response to the previous running argument between Poland and Germany. The French campaign was a response to the fact that France, not Germany, had declared war.

But the Russians had done everything to avoid war, and Hitler

*Hitler at Nuremberg rally*

said quite firmly: 'We shall invade Russia.' Surprisingly enough perhaps, when you think of the alarms of the German generals in the past, this time the German generals did not oppose him. They were overwhelmed by his staggering strategical success against France, and accepted he could do something similar against Russia.

Moreover, like many people in the West, they grossly underrated Russia's resources, manpower and fighting capacity. They agreed with Hitler that Russia would collapse within a month of the invasion. The whole German invasion was conducted in such a slapdash way that, when the time came, in June 1941, a great deal of it was not ready. Slightly over half the German invading forces had to be supplied from French captured equipment, because the German factories had been going along in too easy a way. You must remember that right up until 1943, there was no

*Hitler reviews labour battalions*

*The orator in action*

decline whatsoever in the German standard of life. They could manage both to win wars, so it seemed, and to enjoy all the comforts of peacetime.

Again, whereas against France the generals made detailed plans, no defined plans were made of what they would do when they got into Russia. They were confident that they would simply break through in one place after another, and the Russian armies would all surrender; in July the war would be over.

Some of the expectations proved true. The Russian front did collapse. Hundreds of thousands of Russian soldiers were surrounded and surrendered. By July, it looked as if all the Soviet positions there at the beginning of the war had been shattered. Leningrad, Moscow and the south were all exposed to further attacks, and yet—and this is what baffled them, it was the first sign of hesitation—the Russian armies had not collapsed. The German generals and Hitler met (it was the first time that Hitler

54

had had a conference with his generals since the beginning of the campaign) in late July, and discussed, for about three weeks, whether they should go for Moscow or try to encircle it. It was only in late August that a great encirclement started, and this was in the south. Again, great victories, and hundreds of thousands of Russians surrendering, fronts collapsing, but no decision. Late in the autumn, the drive to Moscow was resumed.

This was the turning-point of the Second World War. In June 1941, Germany was the acknowledged victor, dominant over the whole of Europe. In December 1941, the German forces halted in front of Moscow. They were never to take it.

And from that moment, Hitler appreciated that total victory could not be achieved. On the other hand, he was confident that,

*German entry into Austria*

*Hess, Hitler and Baldur von Schirach at Nuremberg rally, 1938*

56

*Chamberlain, angel of peace*

if the German armies held on in their existing positions, they could renew the campaign next year. Indeed, one English historian has gone so far as to describe this as Hitler's finest hour, when he and he alone breathed resolution into the wretched German troops through the horrors of the bitter Russian winter.

There was an almost complete collapse of the marshals and generals. The commander-in-chief collapsed. No new commander-in-chief was appointed, so that Hitler was first of all head of the supreme command, then he was minister of war, or had replaced the minister of war, and now also commander-in-chief of the army on the Eastern front. From being, as he had been in 1939, a spectator, he was the operative chief. It was his detailed orders on the Eastern front which ran the campaign of 1942, and although on the other fronts that came up later—say, the Italian front in 1943 and the Western, or French, front in 1944—there were commanders-in-chief there, they still had almost daily instructions from Hitler.

It was at this time he became really a recluse, settling down in an underground bunker, running the war far from the front. I think there was only one occasion when he ever went to the front, and only one other attempt at a public appearance—a speech to his Nazi followers in November 1943.

Hitler sounds a most unattractive man, but he could impress people, not only make them fear him, but inspire them again and again. A general faced with the problems of the front flew to Hitler's headquarters determined to impress the truth on him. And after half an hour he came out uplifted and said: 'It's going to be all right. The Führer has said we shall win, and so we shall hold together.'

Hitler's stroke of 1942 was, in a sense, more limited than the three great offensives sweeping right across Russia in 1941. This one was to be a single drive, a drive south-east into the Caucasus and to Stalingrad. Why did Hitler choose Stalingrad? You have

*Entry of German troops into Warsaw, 1939*

*Hitler and Goering in conference, 1939*

only got to look on the map. If the Germans captured Stalingrad, they would hamper, perhaps cut off entirely, the flow of supplies from southern Russia, and particularly from Persia, and the supplies of oil up into central Russia.

I think there was something else. He now saw the war as a personal conflict and believed that, if he could capture Stalingrad, or threaten Stalingrad—the city of Stalin—Stalin would respond to the challenge and, rather like Verdun in the First World War, the Soviet armies would bleed to death. But the Soviet armies were building up their supplies all the time, and new factories were pouring out things. The German achievements in equipment were being everywhere overshadowed.

Stalingrad was the first great disaster on the German side, and it was caused by exactly the same thing which, at the end of 1941, had restored the German army to its preponderant position.

Once more, Hitler issued the order to stand fast. When Stalingrad was encircled, he refused to authorise the withdrawal of the Germans. This was again solely his decision. He believed that, if

*German troops in Paris, 1940*

*Hitler at the Eiffel Tower, 1940*

*Goering surveys the English Channel, 1940*

he gave orders, he would make others so resolute that they would overcome impossible odds. In January 1943, when Stalingrad held out and the German forces surrendered, there was the transformation that Germany was now on the defensive.

Throughout 1943, the defensive was conducted in the east with obstinacy, but it was a defensive all the time, in which the scale of German losses was increasing. And when, in 1944, the Western Allies landed in northern France, there was pressure on both fronts.

Some people speculate about why there was never any consideration of a compromise peace. Some Germans attempted it: some negotiated with the Western powers, some negotiated with the Russians. Hitler, so far as we can tell, never contemplated this. He had formed a picture. For him, although the war could never be won, it was not necessary that it should be lost. His other great inspiration was the Japanese attack on the Americans at

Pearl Harbor, which made him feel that, over at the other end of the world, there would be an ally who would stand by him.

For this and for no other reason, he plunged, at the end of 1941, the very time of his Moscow disasters, into the Japanese War. He declared war on America and thus solved President Roosevelt's greatest problem—how to get the Americans into the war. Hitler made at this time the most extraordinary remark: 'We have chosen the wrong side; we ought to be the allies of the Anglo-Saxon powers. But providence has imposed on us this world-historical mistake.' And, in a sense, you could argue that all his campaigns after the first defeats were a world-historical mistake.

Was there sense in it? In a perverted way, yes. Hitler was confident that, sooner or later, the two Western powers, Britain and America, and Soviet Russia, the Eastern power, would quarrel. They would quarrel territorially because they had different

*The War Lords in conference, 1941*

outlooks. They would quarrel politically because one side was capitalistic democracy, the other side was communist. And, at a certain moment, the two extremes, instead of battering away against Germany, would start bidding for German aid. Germany would be transformed from the enemy of all the world into the ally, the key power, which would swing the whole world situation differently.

Right up to the end, when things were going catastrophically, Hitler could give only one order: 'Hang on, hang on.' As a strategist, he still had great strokes of offensive genius, particularly at first, but then also in Russia up till 1943, when there was his gambler's throw. There was one other gambler's throw, which is difficult to estimate. Right till the very end, Hitler believed that some new miracle weapon would be discovered which would tip the scale. We now know that most of this was bluff.

*Hitler and Eva Braun at home, 1941*

*German troops in the Russian snow*

For instance, German scientists had not got anywhere near the atomic bomb, although they knew the methods. Later on, they were to boast that they delayed deliberately, but the truth is that Hitler was not interested at that time. He thought Germany could win without it, and, when he began to talk of new weapons, it was too late.

He became, in the end, physically an absolutely broken man. And yet we have descriptions of people visiting him in the bunker in Berlin—now German territory had been squeezed in—with his left arm shattered, at any rate crippled, following a bomb going off in his meeting-room in July 1944, trembling all over, dragging his feet, hardly able to speak, and yet there was the same magic effect—the inspiration with which people would come away.

*German aircraft abandoned after El Alamein*

*The ruins of Hamburg, 1943*

Generals who commanded phantom armies, armies which did not exist, were now reporting. Yet Hitler would take them into the map-room to show them where this imaginary army or that imaginary army would strike against the Russians, and, for a time, they believed it. Few of them could break loose from Hitler's magnetic personality and from the promise of victory which he held out.

At the very end, he was left alone against the Russian forces. He dismissed most of his staff, kept only his most loyal followers, and lived in a fantasy where he was still sending out these messages. When other German leaders—Goering, for instance, who was well away from Hitler—hinted that he would now try to

*Hitler's only inspection of bomb damage, 1944*

negotiate a peace, even if it was a peace of surrender, Hitler simply struck him off and ordered that he be arrested.

At the very last, he came to recognise that the war had been lost—that the Western powers and Soviet Russia were not going to quarrel. There was an extraordinary epilogue. Hitler had been very much a man on his own. He had no confidants, he had no friends. You can read what is called his table-talk. But it was, in fact, Hitler in his military train during the war, sitting around after a meal, haranguing the generals endlessly on his past, on German history, on how he had risen to the top, on philosophic reflections. But it is quite obvious that he had no friendly connections with any of these generals or with any of the others; he treated Goering as an amusing acquaintance. He was a solitary man, though he sometimes accepted, of course, advice from others, sometimes decisions. It is, I think, true, for instance, that the terrible massacre of the Jews was inspired more by Himmler

*Hitler's last inspection of his last troops, 1945*

*In the bunker, 1945*

*Berchtesgaden 20 years after*

than by Hitler, though Hitler took it up.

Now, at the last moment, with only a few hours to live, he married Eva Braun, who had been his mistress for many years. He had said: 'You can't have a mistress coming between a Führer and the German people.' Now she got this last consolation of being his wife for a few hours.

The following day, after an affecting farewell, and his writing his last testament, he and Eva Braun withdrew. She took poison and also Hitler shot her, to make sure. He probably shot himself, but he may have taken poison. His body has never been found.

With this death and disappearance, Hitler performed a final service to the German people—he carried with him into obscurity the responsibility for the world war and the guilt for the crimes and atrocities with which it had been accompanied. As a result, the German people were left innocent.

# 3

# CHURCHILL

# Churchill

In 1932, when Lady Astor was in Russia, she told Stalin that Churchill was finished: 'a busted flush' in Beaverbrook's words. Stalin did not agree. He said that if the English were ever in trouble, they might need the old warhorse again. And this is exactly what happened. Stalin's phrase was an appropriate one. Churchill managed somehow to carry the aura of being an old warrior brought back into the field; yet with it, he had an almost youthful zest.

Churchill was much the most experienced of the 20th-century war lords, in the sense that he had been in politics for a very long time. He had been in the House of Commons, on and off, from 1900; he became a cabinet minister as early as 1908; he had been at the head of almost every great department of state except the Foreign Office. On the other hand, he had had long periods of failure: in the late 1930s, he was extremely unpopular—at any rate, not highly regarded. Indeed, late in 1938, he talked of retiring from public life. He said: 'My career is a failure; it is finished. There is nothing more to offer.' But, a few months after the beginning of the Second World War, he began a new career, though one which was enormously shaped by what had gone before.

His new career began in May 1940, after the unsuccessful British campaign in Norway—a campaign, ironically, for which Churchill was mainly responsible and the failures of which were due more to him than to Chamberlain, the prime minister, who

*Churchill, parliamentary candidate at Manchester in 1908*

was actually discredited, Nevertheless, Churchill became prime minister.

Nowadays, looking back, we think of Churchill as the leader of a united nation which persisted wholeheartedly in the war from 1940 until 1945. That is not how it seemed at the time. In 1940 there was still a lot of disagreement under the surface. Many Conservative members of Parliament resented the way in which Chamberlain had been pushed aside, and when Churchill first appeared in the House of Commons to make his famous speech about blood, toil, tears and sweat, he was cheered from the Labour benches only. The Conservatives remained silent until Chamberlain came in.

Some weeks later, an influential journalist warned Chamberlain that this behaviour was giving a bad impression. The Conservative chief whip told off his chaps, and then, at a signal of the whip's handkerchief, they cheered Churchill. But it was a cheer which sprang from calculation; it was not until much later that Churchill became the undisputed leader of the country. Even then, he was often challenged. He actually had a vote of no confidence moved against him, in July 1942. Although only 25 MPs voted for it, it represented a much wider spread of criticism.

Churchill had to be on his best behaviour. He had to remember the failures of the past—failures which were due to his too-great enterprise, to his enthusiasm for victory. He once said, when contemplating some risky course: 'Remember, I have the medals of Antwerp, Gallipoli, Norway and elsewhere pinned on my chest.' In other words, though he could not resist an enterprise, he sometimes cautiously hung back.

He was, undoubtedly, a war lord. He was not a dictator, of course: he had arrived at his position in the constitutional way, following the House of Commons's loss of confidence in Chamberlain. He presided over a small war cabinet. He also introduced an entirely new rank. He made himself minister of defence, of which he said that the changes were more real than apparent. By becoming this, he could exercise a completely undefined authority over the whole sphere of war. Moreover, he controlled an institution which had never existed in British history before, which did not exist in most other countries; did not exist in Germany, for example. There was a chiefs-of-staff committee, combining the heads of the three services, which, in theory, at any

*Churchill, Secretary for War, visiting British troops on the Rhine, 1919*

*Dunkirk, waiting for evacuation*

rate, directed the war. In practice, Churchill did a good deal of the direction himself. He was, unmistakably, the outstanding minister, as far as public opinion went. Everyone knew this was Churchill's government, that he was the one person who mattered.

Nevertheless, it is surprising how rarely he actually imposed his will on generals and chiefs of staff. He once said (and it is a most delightful and characteristic remark): 'All I asked was compliance with my wishes after reasonable discussion.' It was not so much that he dictated or that he ordered: he wore people down.

He himself was inexhaustible. He could argue and argue, and a general or a chief of staff who was less ready to go on with these wearisome arguments until late at night would flag. But those who stood up to him—for example, Alan Brooke, the Chief of the Imperial General Staff for much of the war—were able to resist his urgings. Though Alan Brooke expressed his exasperation in his private diary, he never did so in public, and the same, I think, is true of the other chiefs of staff. There is one case, however, which I will mention later, when Admiral Pound, who was first sea lord, was driven into something that he hesitated about, with disastrous consequences.

Churchill combined extreme impatience and a readiness to try

*Dunkirk, British and French troops on the beach*

*Dunkirk, back home*

new ideas with an ultimate willingness to be restrained. Roosevelt, who was often sceptical about him, said: 'You know, Winston has 100 ideas every day, and one of them is almost sure to be right.' But Churchill did not mind; he would produce another 99 the next day. He was sometimes cast down, not so much by defeat, but by his own calculations and hopes going wrong. He had very gloomy periods, but, predominantly, he would rise again, with new ideas, with new enthusiasms, and would, as all his associates agreed, carry them with him— persuade them to share his enthusiasm.

He liked to think he was a tyrant. When someone told him that Hitler bullied his generals, Churchill replied: 'I do the same.' And if the generals were at all weak, then he would dismiss them. He had a long record, far greater in length than Lloyd George's in the First World War, of dismissing generals who had failed, often when the failure was by no means their own fault. He sacked Wavell from command in North Africa, although Wavell was, I suppose, the most distinguished British general in the early days of the war. He sacked Auchinleck. Someone has calculated that, at one time or another, he proposed to dismiss every one of the great admirals of war, though he did not succeed in every case. He proposed, at one time or another, to sack Cunningham; Somerville; Forbes, the commander of the Home Fleet; Tovey, his successor; and Harwood. He disliked failure or hesitation and had a faith that, if you went on sacking long enough, it would come right. And, in a sense, it did.

Churchill's first great contribution was ensuring that, after the fall of France, the war would go on. At the time, the impression was given that everyone was united over this. We now know that, in the secrecy of the cabinet, during the last days of May 1940, the possibility of a negotiated peace, with Mussolini as the mediator, and a new Munich, was seriously discussed and pressed by Halifax (I cannot say strongly pressed, because Halifax never did

*Air Marshal Sir Hugh Dowding, victor in the Battle of Britain*

79

anything strongly). Even Chamberlain hesitated. It was the two Labour men, Attlee and Greenwood, who were firm on the other side—and Churchill, who said that it would be impossible. The prospect of a negotiated peace did not, I think, really disappear until after victory in the Battle of Britain.

The Battle of Britain was, for this country, the decisive battle of the war; it ensured that Britain would not be invaded. It was won by Air Chief Marshal Sir Hugh Dowding. His conduct of the battle, his securing that Fighter Command should be strong enough, the skilful way in which, with the assistance of his air marshals, he directed Fighter Command, won a battle which was as great, as decisive and, in a sense, as glorious in our history as the Battle of

*Battle of Britain 'scramble'*

Trafalgar. But, at an earlier stage, Dowding had contradicted Churchill. He had opposed sending fighter squadrons to France; so, the moment the Battle of Britain was won, Dowding was relieved of his command, and passed into obscurity.

There were others whom Churchill did not forgive, but Dowding, I think, is the most striking; and it was the open going against him which Churchill did not like.

Broadly, British strategy in the Second World War—though, no doubt, it was based on prewar events and on the proposals of the chiefs of staff—was decided by Churchill. He had a great, though not an unquestioning, faith in bombing. When strategical bombing of Germany started, it was largely for the reason that, if

*Battle of Britain: war in the skies*

*Pilots and their Hurricanes*

we don't do this, there is nothing we can do. Remember, after all, that on any large scale, British and German troops did not fight large battles between 1940 and 1943. For those three years there was a pause—a war in theory more than in practice—and British bombing was one way to show that the British were in the war The bombing campaign was certainly sustained by Churchill, though he was readier than others to recognise that it did not achieve all that it was said it would do. Bombing did not win the war unaided by land armies.

The second campaign, which was more characteristic and did more not only to shape the British pattern of war but to absorb Churchill's attention, was the British campaign in the Mediterranean. It was begun in July 1940 again on the very simple ground that there was nothing else to do. The British had been turned out of the continent, there was a British army in Egypt: how could they fight unless they stayed in Egypt? If you ask what the Mediterranean campaign was about, why the British were ever in the Mediterranean, one can give the simple answer of the Second World War, as of the First on some occasions: they were there because they were there—because they were there. And being there, then they had better stay there and fight. One of Churchill's most courageous decisions was to send reinforcements out to the Mediterranean even before the Battle of Britain was over. But, once there, more and more British resources were drawn in. It was not until 1944 that the British forces were able to return to the continent itself.

There was a positive side to Churchill's interest in the Mediterranean. He had always been fascinated by it. For him, it represented the deepest legacy of imperial strategy as it had been from the time of Nelson to that of the First World War, with its campaigns in Palestine and Mesopotamia. He also continued to hold the belief he had held in the First World War which inspired the catastrophic expedition to Gallipoli—that there was from the Mediterranean a back door into Europe. He sometimes referred to it as the soft underbelly of the Axis.

*Fighter Command: the plotting room*

*Bracken, Churchill and Mrs Churchill inspect war damage*

This was a very curious idea. Churchill was a great one for maps and, if he had looked at one of the Mediterranean, he would have seen that the countries by which you could penetrate into Europe, either Italy or the Balkan countries, are not a soft underbelly at all; they are very hard, mountainous countries. And we know as a fact that the Allied armies never managed to reach Germany from the south before the war ended. The Mediterranean campaign was much more a campaign against Italy, which was of no importance, than it was against Germany.

Churchill also had the belief that Turkey was crying out to go to war against Germany, and all it needed was a little encouragement from Great Britain. This belief was totally mistaken.

Though it was essential, no doubt, to have a war in the

*Churchill on his first day as Prime Minister*

Mediterranean in order to show that the British were still winning battles (and, of course, sometimes losing them), as a positive achievement towards turning strategy against Germany, it turned out to be disappointing. But it was Churchill's obsession that he must do something, and he often snatched at historical tactics which had once been successful, but were now out of date.

Churchill was very historical, in the sense that he could look back. I read the other day a description of him in August 1940, when the Germans were about to invade, and some of his colleagues, not actually the chiefs of staff, were gathered with him

*Churchill and Eden his loyal acolyte*

*The Chiefs of Staff in conference*

one evening. They thought he would discuss the German invasion, because he said: 'I want to discuss the problems of invasion.' But he turned to the invasion by William the Conqueror in 1066, and spent the entire evening discussing the problems which William had faced and the reasons the Anglo-Saxons, led by Harold, had failed to repel the invasion. For him, in a sense, the problem of 1066 was as living as the problems of 1940. History was part of his life.

On the other hand he was very up-to-date. In the First World War he had initiated the use of the tank. Strangely enough, he did not appreciate, at first, in the Second World War, the enormous transformation this had caused. He confessed in 1940, about the French army, that he had had no idea that a decisive victory, such as the Germans gained over the French, could be achieved with tank forces. He often took time to catch up, and his appearance presented this mixture of old and new. Sometimes, he appeared in the House of Commons wearing a frockcoat—a garment which had gone out, I suppose, with Edward VII. Sometimes, he went round in a siren suit, in which, with his baby face, he looked like an overgrown child bouncing around in rompers; and he had the

87

*General Percival on his way to surrender at Singapore*

same exuberance of spirit.

His phraseology was a mixture of high rhetoric and humour. His speeches sound better now perhaps than they did at the time, when they did not always come across very well, though they were undoubtedly inspiring. The fact that he was always so lively also brought inspiration to others.

He made many mistakes. All war lords make mistakes. Churchill's mistakes were the mistakes of hurrying too much, of wanting victory too soon and wanting it with inadequate means. Historians still debate whether the expedition to Greece, in April 1941, was a mistake. It was certainly extremely unsuccessful. Other little ideas, such as when he would send off troops and they would be lost, sprang from this impatience to do something. Nevertheless, on most of the great issues, though not on all, he was restrained.

I suppose his greatest mistake was his refusal to take seriously the danger in the Far East; yet one might say he had to refuse. If he had concentrated on the Far East before the Japanese attacked, the Mediterranean might well have been lost. He said at one point that he did not realise the weakness of Singapore: 'I ought to have asked; my advisers ought to have told me.' Well, I am sorry to say that the records show his advisers told him, and Churchill pushed their warnings aside, with a gesture of the old imperial greatness which was no longer relevant. He said: 'The little yellow men will never dare to challenge the might of the British Empire.' But, in the autumn of 1941, the might of the British

*El Alamein: the artillery barrage*

*Churchill, Montgomery and Alan Brooke*

Empire did not exist in the Far East. He sent out a battleship and a battlecruiser to be what he called 'a vague menace'. It was the occasion when Admiral Pound was overruled; and it was a catastrophe—the two ships were lost. It was Churchill all over; if he could not do something effective, he would do something ineffective.

The one area in which he had had little experience was, I think, in some ways, the area in which he was most successful. He had been everything except foreign secretary, but it was in his conduct of foreign affairs that he showed endless, or almost endless, patience. This patience was sorely tried by General de Gaulle, whom he referred to as 'my Cross of Lorraine'; yet it was Churchill, more than anyone else, who kept de Gaulle going and ensured that de Gaulle went back to a united, liberated France. But most of all, Churchill's co-operation, his linking up with the

*Allied landing at Anzio, January 1944*

two great allies, the United States and Soviet Russia, was the highest point of his career and the time when he was both most courageous and most creative.

From the time when he became prime minister, all his thoughts had been pinned on getting the Americans into the war. And he describes how, when the Japanese bombed Pearl Harbor and destroyed part of the American Pacific fleet, he nevertheless slept peacefully, because America had come into the war. He ends his account of Pearl Harbor by remarking: 'So we had won after all.' It was absolutely clear, from the moment the United States were allies, that there would be, as indeed there was, total victory over the Axis powers.

Churchill exaggerated American generosity. For the United States, for Roosevelt himself, Great Britain was an essential element in strategy. But the Americans also had an exaggerated idea, which they learnt from Churchill himself, of the grandeur of the British Empire, and they were determined to squeeze it down.

Churchill had been extremely anti-Bolshevik; he had run the wars of intervention. Nevertheless, from the first moment that Soviet Russia was attacked, he committed himself wholeheartedly to the Russian side. People have argued that, later on, he took precautions against Soviet victory. I don't think so. He was apprehensive about Soviet victory, but, until the end of the war, he remained faithful to the Soviet alliance. He depicted his relations between Soviet Russia and the United States at Teheran when he wrote: 'There I sat with the great Russian bear on one side of me with paws outstretched, and, on the other side, the

*D-day, 6th June 1944*

*After the flying bomb, Clapham*

*Churchill at Cherbourg, 1944*

*Churchill at Yalta, 1945*

great American buffalo. Between the two sat the poor little English donkey, who was the only one who knew the right way home.' That was a realistic judgement. Compared with Soviet Russia and the United States, Great Britain was perhaps a poor little English donkey, though an essential one, and the only one, the only country, together with the Dominions, who carried the burden of war from beginning to end.

Churchill imagined a great future for the British Empire and yet—and this, again, was characteristic of him—he recognised the contradictions between his vision of the grandeur of the old

*Churchill in Hitler's chair*

empire and the realities of the present.

In his first speech to the Commons after he became prime minister, he defined his policy as 'victory at all costs', and he made it quite clear that he meant victory even if the British Empire were to perish; victory even if we were to become an impoverished country. He said: 'I've only one aim in life: that is to defeat Hitler. That makes things very simple for me.' Though he had other aims in life—to preserve the British Empire and the conservative social structure in which he had grown up—yet, essentially, they were eclipsed by the other thing that, whatever

95

sacrifices were necessary for the war, he was ready to make them and recognised that Great Britain should make them.

His achievements far eclipsed his failures. Even on the personal side, though he cleared away many generals, he raised up several successful ones. Montgomery was not, in fact, a discovery of his and, in the early days, they worked uneasily together. But once Montgomery offered him what no other British general had offered him until that time—victory—Churchill accepted this somewhat difficult personality.

At a time when his physical powers were waning, Churchill

*Churchill's State funeral*

*Churchill's coffin leaving St. Paul's*

still continued to survey the whole field of war, and even the most critical would hesitate to say that anyone could have taken his place. In this strange people's war, this war of the worlds, there was this old-fashioned character with his cigar—rarely, I may say, smoked. What Churchill did, in Beaverbrook's words, was to smoke matches. There was, in Churchill, a combination of the profound strategist, the experienced man and the actor. Not always the tragic actor; there was a rich comedy about him as well. No other war leader, I think, had the same depth of personal fascination as Churchill.

One historian has called Churchill, I think rightly, the saviour of his country. And, certainly, his country recognised him as such. When he died, he was given a state funeral, as had been given to the other two great saviours of their country, Nelson and Wellington. It was characteristic of him that he worked out a great many of the details of it himself. But something unrehearsed happened during the closing moments of the last part of the funeral procession through London: the loading-cranes along the banks of the Thames were dipped in final salute. His body was then taken to Blaydon and put in a humble grave beside his father. In this way, he combined, to the end, imperial greatness with human simplicity.

# 4

# STALIN

# Stalin

Most people, I suppose, regard Stalin as a monster. Khrushchev said of him: 'Like Peter the Great, he fought barbarism with barbarism.' Yet, for a tyrant, he was curiously unobtrusive, almost unassertive. During the Bolshevik revolution, though he played a part, it was a modest one. Another participant, looking back, said: 'All I remember of Stalin is that he seemed like a grey blur—somebody you would hardly notice against the landscape.'

Of all the war lords I have talked about, or am going to talk about, Stalin was the only one who saw high command in the First World War or, rather, in the wars of intervention which followed it. He distinguished himself by his defence of Tsaritsyn, which as a result became known as Stalingrad. He also served in Poland. He was extremely insubordinate, taking little notice of the instructions he received from the commissar for war, Trotsky. He even took little notice of the instructions he received from Lenin, the leader of the revolution. He went his own way and stood up for himself: not conduct he would have tolerated from his own generals in the Second World War.

It was not until 1928, some ten years after the Bolshevik revolution, that Stalin manoeuvred himself into supreme power. His title remained general secretary of the Communist Party and, officially, he had no governmental position; but there can be no doubt that from 1928 he was dictator of the Soviet Union.

His rule became increasingly harsh. He arrested people by the thousand, perhaps by the million. He liquidated, as the phrase

*Stalin in 1919, 'a grey blur'*

was, all his old political associates; he liquidated practically the whole high command of the Soviet army. So in 1939, when the Second World War began, Stalin stood alone, puzzled, suspicious, with nobody whom he respected, nobody whose opinions he accepted, and hardly aware of the world outside the Soviet Union. But he did have a profound anxiety: that if there were a great European war against Germany in which the Soviet Union was involved, she would have to do most of the fighting. And so it proved, for, from the time the Russians came into the war, they contended, most of the time, with four-fifths of the German army, and never with less than three-quarters. There are those who speak slightingly of Stalin making a non-aggression pact with Hitler in August 1939. But his motive was to keep his country out of war for as long as he could. Also, he misjudged: he believed that Great Britain and France would keep a western front going for a long time, thus giving the Russians time to prepare for war.

When France fell and Great Britain was then on her own, Sta-

*Stalin and Maxim Gorky*

lin believed—indeed, it was an obsession—that Hitler would not attack the Russians until he had finished with Britain. Thus, he thought he would have enough time to prepare for the attack.

Undoubtedly, Stalin was anticipating a German attack from the time that France fell, in June 1940. Unfortunately, many of his preparations were misplaced. He believed and, for a long time continued to believe, that an all-out offensive was the only answer to invasion. He grouped the Russian armies all along the western frontier, so that they could begin their victorious march to Berlin; in fact, they had to wait four years for that.

In the early months of 1941, somebody has calculated, Stalin received no fewer than 76 separate warnings that Germany was about to invade Russia. They came from the American gov-

*Lenin alone in his chair; the picture of Stalin was imposed later*

*Generalissimo Stalin*

*Molotov signs the*
*Nazi-Soviet pact*

ernment, from the British government, from Stalin's own secret agents all over Europe and from practical indications of the mobilisation of the German forces. But Stalin said: 'Hitler is going to threaten us, he is going to exact greater concessions from us; but, as long as he has Great Britain to contend with, he will not invade us.'

Even when, on 22 June 1941, German troops were actually crossing the Russian frontier, he refused, at first, to allow his generals to fight back. And when, in the course of the day, the whole Russian front collapsed, the only reply they could get from Moscow was: 'The boss knows best.' All through the summer of 1941, the boss did not know best. But Stalin was to learn, though belatedly, from experience, and in the later days of the war the boss really did know best.

*Stalin cautiously takes a walk*

*Marshal Zhukov, the greatest General of World War II*

It is fascinating how Stalin piled one position of authority on the other. Just before the German invasion, he took for the first time a political position. He became chairman of the Council of People's Commissars, or, as we would say, prime minister. When the war started, he first of all appointed himself commissar for defence, then he appointed himself commander-in-chief, then he appointed himself supreme commander. He dominated, first of all, the General Staff, which was composed of generals. He dominated the Military Council of Defence, which was composed mainly of satellite politicians. He also dominated the political body which ran internal affairs. He was even chairman of the committee which, later on, issued directions to the partisans. Every line of policy ran, had to run, through Stalin's study. Stalin alone made every great decision throughout the war and many of the small ones, too.

106

Stalin did not worry about tactics. He perhaps did not worry enough about the details of equipment. But he grasped the necessity for tanks and for aircraft, though the Russian aircraft, I think, were never of the highest quality. He also grasped, quite early in the war, that in the vast spaces of Russia the greatest resource which would bring victory was the ability to move. So in April 1942, he told an American representative: 'We don't want any more tanks; what we want are trucks.' And if you ask why, later in the war, the Russians were able to move quickly from one spot to another, it was because of the thousands, perhaps tens of thousands, of American trucks for which Stalin had asked. Now, that was a wonderful stroke of penetration: to appreciate how the preparations for war had been out of balance; that, unless he could deliver the chaps to the front, no amount of tanks would make the decision.

Stalin continued for most of 1941 to be obsessed with his belief that to be on the offensive was the only answer. It brought upon the Soviet armies greater catastrophes than any other armies have ever known. Between June 1941 and the tailing-off of the

*Taking the salute on the Red Square Moscow, 7th November 1941*

German offensive, which came in October, the Russians lost something like four million dead, and at least two million Russians were made German prisoners-of-war, many of them later being murdered. It was the inexhaustible human resources of Soviet Russia which kept her going. At one time, Halder, the German chief of staff, said: 'We estimated that we should contend

107

*Street barricades in Moscow, 1942*

with 180 Russian divisions; we have already counted 360.' Many
of the Russians were ill-trained reservists, but there were also
crack troops. When Stalin, immensely daring, brought troops
from the Far East, he calculated that Japan, once she got locked
in war against America, would not turn against Russia. These
forces helped to save Moscow. The halt of the German armies
before Moscow, when they were stopped and defeated for the first
time by the Russian armies, with Marshal Zhukov in command,
marked the real turning-point of the war in Russia.

The German invasion of Russia, just like the German invasion
of France, was *blitzkrieg;* it aimed at producing a decision
immediately. The Germans thought they had produced the decision by the end of July. Then they recognised they had not. They
aimed again—and German troops actually saw the towers of the
Kremlin gleaming in the winter sun; they reached a tram ter-
minus in the Moscow suburbs. There they were stopped and,
during the winter, were driven back.

Stalin over-estimated his successes. In December 1941, he told

Eden, who was then visiting Moscow: 'In a few months, I shall have troops to join you in the Far East.' In fact, he was going to have to wait another three years at least before he could envisage sending troops there.

The Russian counter-offensive petered out. Both sides prepared for a further offensive. Here again, Stalin misjudged. His great mistake was to insist on trying to disturb the German plans by an offensive of his own. This was the Russian offensive of March to May 1942 against Kharkov, which was catastrophic and opened the whole of south Russia to German invasion forces. Stalin again refused to allow any kind of retreats and, as a result, most of the Russian armies there were lost. But this was the

*Anti-tank obstacles Moscow, 1942*

last time that this mistake was made. In the summer of 1942, when the Russian armies were battered by the Germans, they retreated.

Stalin did not become less fierce to his commanders. He could be both fierce and then winning. On one occasion, he complained that Zhukov had not been sufficiently offensive. Indeed, they had a fierce argument in the Kremlin, and Zhukov finally said: 'Well, I'd better resign then as chief of staff.' Stalin replied: 'Yes, you better had and go and take command at the front.' Zhukov was the only man who dared to argue with Stalin, and he went on

*The streets of Stalingrad, 1942*

*One German soldier who crossed the Volga*

arguing with him on this occasion. Stalin suddenly changed his whole manner. He smiled at Zhukov and said: 'Comrade general, don't be too upset, these things happen to anybody in war, but your career has been successful. Now let's sit down and have a cup of tea.' And with that he dispatched Zhukov to the front. Stalin had these strange ups and downs. Sometimes, in the early days of the war, he was savage. He would ring up perhaps half-a-dozen generals whose armies had retreated during the day, and tell them to come to Moscow at once. Immediately on arrival in Moscow, they were brought before a court martial and then, in the evening, shot. Stalin was the only war lord of the Second World War who shot his generals for failure in the field. Hitler, of course, shot some generals who conspired against him, but that was something very different.

No wonder, then, that Stalin's generals were all his absolute subordinates. There was never an instance of one directly defying him. There were some generals who argued, some who evaded, but the combination of terror and of loyalty maintained Stalin's supremacy. After all, he was the boss, the centre of everything.

Simply from the physical point of view, it is amazing that any one man could have accomplished the things he did. Unlike any commander ever known, Stalin literally ran every front himself. He had three great fronts: one in Leningrad; one in the centre at Moscow; and one in the south, which went down to Stalingrad. Because they were all in his own empire, he could communicate with them. He spoke to the three chief commanders for a long

*Soviet tanks moving up to the battle of Kursk*

*German troops in retreat*

time on the telephone every evening. He issued the next day's orders to them. He sent them the details of the troops and supplies he could provide. At the same time, he had under his hand the running of Russian internal affairs—concerning himself with all kinds of civil problems, economic problems, personally presiding over that vast shift of industry to behind the Urals. Very often, too, he rang up lower-ranking generals, either to encourage them, or, sometimes, to rebuke them. If there was a query, if even one of the marshals doubted him, he would tell him to come to Moscow and the whole thing would be sorted out.

Stalin's personal control of his country's war effort was unique. Hitler directed Germany's war effort, but through a considerable staff. And very often his chiefs of staff, like Keitel and Jodl, issued orders without consulting him. For a great deal of the time he was

*Soviet troops on the attack*

*Russian troops entering a German town*

not in direct personal communication with his commanders-in-chief. But there was never a moment from the time when the Russian fronts became something like stabilised that Stalin was not in complete personal control.

For Stalin, I think that 13-14 September 1942 was the decisive time. It was then that he conferred with the two generals on the southern front, when the German armies had already reached the outskirts of Stalingrad. When he was discussing how Stalingrad could be defended, he heard them murmuring together in the corner about something else. He staggered them by the quickness with which he picked up what they were saying: 'What's that you say, counter-offensive?' And they replied: 'Well, yes, Comrade Stalin, we had thought that instead of just holding our own, we

*Churchill, Stalin and Molotov in Moscow, October 1944*

*Churchill, Roosevelt and Stalin at Yalta*

could cut the Germans off.' Stalin meditated and then said: 'But this would mean a long delay.' 'Yes,' they agreed, 'two months.' And he told them to go ahead with the counter-offensive. But he was often impatient, often anxious. He would become apprehensive in the evenings and ring up to say: 'You're going to be too slow: the Germans are going to take Stalingrad.' Then he would ring up again the next morning and say: 'Well, if you think it can be done, let it go ahead.'

Just as, in May 1940, the Germans pulled off a wonderful strategic stroke at Sedan, and just as in December 1941, the Japanese pulled off a wonderful stroke at Pearl Harbor, so the Russian counter-offensive, which was launched on 19 November 1942, was a strategical stroke of the greatest significance. A stroke far greater than the Russians expected. They thought they would take 90,000 prisoners; in fact, they took over a quarter of a million. The whole German front was shattered.

The following summer, there was confirmation that Stalin had

*German prisoners in Russia*

learned patience. Once more, there was a field of combat between the Germans and the Russians—at Kursk, a very awkward bulge, or salient. In the old days, Stalin would have said: 'Attack, break out.' His generals persuaded him to wait. It was the Germans who attacked, and it was their army which was defeated. Without doubt, the battle of Kursk was the decisive battle of the eastern front. From that moment on, the German armies lost their superiority. Incidentally, Kursk was the greatest tank battle ever known, unless we count some of the battles which took place in the last Middle Eastern war; but the Russian battles included vast infantry forces.

Now Stalin was pursuing, cautiously, a series of victories. The Russians never had a defeat, though they often stopped. The whole concept of Stalin's strategy was not to go driving ahead as the Germans, despite obstacles, had done. Every time he came up against an obstacle, he stopped. This, among other things, produced the tragedy of Warsaw. The Russian armies had already stopped outside Warsaw when there was a revolt in the city against its German occupiers. It would have demanded resources which, at that time, the Russians had not got to penetrate Warsaw.

At this time, too, Stalin became an international statesman. Until 1939, when von Ribbentrop, the German foreign minister, came to Moscow, Stalin had never met a statesman of the first rank. He did not meet anyone else until Eden came and then Churchill. When he met Churchill, it was the first time Stalin had

*Captured German standards on display in the Red Square*

ever met a man of his own rank: a man who was also prime minister and of great power and character.

There is perhaps nothing more fascinating in the war than the meeting of these two men, apparently so alien to one another in outlook. Churchill got his blow in very quickly by saying: 'You know, I was very hostile to you. I conducted the war of intervention against you after the First World War. I hope you've forgiven me.' Stalin, who incidentally was educated for the priesthood, said, very characteristically: 'It is for God to forgive.'

*Soviet troops enter Danzig, March 1945*

*Soviet tanks in Warsaw, 1945*

The two rowed at each other. On one occasion when Stalin had provoked Churchill, Churchill began to answer him in denouncing terms, and the interpreter could not keep up with what he was saying. Stalin said: 'Don't bother. It doesn't matter what he's saying; I like his spirit.' For a time, at any rate, there was an intimacy.

The two agreed on one thing. People often talk about Stalin's political designs during the Second World War: they seem to think that communists never stop thinking about political conquests. In my opinion, Stalin could have said what Churchill said: 'I have only one aim in life—that is to beat Hitler. This makes everything simple for me.'

Stalin, far more, after all, than Churchill, had every reason to want to beat Hitler. He had lost, or was to lose, 20 million Soviet

*The Red Flag flies over the Reichstag*

people. People sometimes said there would be a compromise peace between Soviet Russia and Germany. This was inconceivable. The Russians, and Stalin personally, were set on total defeat, on exacting the unconditional surrender of the Germans, long before Roosevelt formulated this.

At the two great international meetings, first in Teheran in 1943 and then at Yalta in 1945, when Stalin, Churchill and Roosevelt conferred together, there was about Stalin a single-mindedness of purpose—to win the war and make Soviet Russia secure thereafter. Roosevelt's mind was full of all kinds of optimistic ideas for the future. Churchill's mind, though very set on the war, was also full of the aspirations of the British Empire.

OPPOSITE *Soviet troops commemorate Stalingrad, May 1945*

*Soviet tanks in Berlin, 1945*

Stalin alone was single-minded in planning victory.

A number of those who were at the conferences remarked on the fact that both Churchill and Roosevelt brought with them a whole host of advisers; also that a lot of information had to be provided for them by their chiefs of staff or whoever it might be. Stalin came with just two or three people whom he would sometimes ask for information; but he could do all the negotiating, he could discuss all the military problems, he could discuss all the political problems and had an absolutely tight grasp of them. Whatever he had been in earlier years, he grew up into being a statesman; one who, without doubt, was totally devoted to the interests of his own country, but also of very great gifts and, in some ways, of considerable sentiment and responsiveness.

There were many who were struck by the way in which Stalin could relax. Mind you, he was set on victory, and he was always,

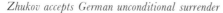

*Zhukov accepts German unconditional surrender*

*Uneasy friendship: Churchill, Truman and Stalin at Potsdam, 1945*

in some ways, a savage. When he said that he thought 50,000 German officers should be shot immediately at the end of the war, this was not a joke, though he subsequently made out that it was. It is really how he felt.

A more trivial instance of his sense of humour occurred at a large party attended by a number of generals and diplomats and others. Stalin called out to one of the generals: 'Bulganin, bring out the machine-guns; let us liquidate the diplomats.' This was his form of fun. He could be quick and sympathetic in talking about it, but also in this brutal way.

Stalin had not envisaged anything at the end of the war except that Soviet Russia should be made stronger and more secure. As long as the war was on, right up to the defeat of Japan, he accepted co-operation with the Western powers. Whether he ever entertained the vision of a permanent co-operation of East and West is, I think, difficult to say. You could ask the same about the others: Churchill, later on, was to claim that he had become disillusioned quite early.

Stalin, I think, assumed, as so many people do, that the relations based on war would go on when the war was over: that there would still be the same feeling of 'Well, we must agree because we're allies in a great war.' But, of course, what happened is that, when the war was over, there was no longer the same intensity of need to agree. And Stalin was very quick to respond suspiciously.

At the Potsdam conference, there was still the appearance of friendship, but then no more. The Cold War, whether started by him or by the Americans—it does not matter who started it—shaped Stalin's outlook.

We know comparatively little about his last years. He became increasingly suspicious and the gifts and brilliance which he had shown appeared to vanish. Indeed, many people think, in the end, he became mad with suspicion, and was proposing a vast new liquidation.

When he died, he was treated as one of the greatest heroes Soviet Russia had ever known, but thereafter he was lowered and degraded. At first, his remains were placed beside those of Lenin; nowadays, though, they have a more modest position under the Kremlin wall.

The last word, perhaps, goes to Averell Harriman, who was American ambassador to Moscow during much of the Second World War. He found Stalin better informed than Roosevelt, more realistic than Churchill—perhaps the most effective of the war lords.

# 5

# ROOSEVELT

# Roosevelt

Franklin Delano Roosevelt was the odd man out among the war lords of the Second World War. While all the others had seen military service in one form or another 20 years earlier, Roosevelt was totally civilian. During the First World War, he had held the assistant secretaryship of the American navy, but this was a political appointment. Nevertheless, it made him regard the navy thereafter as his special service, to the degree that, during the Second World War, General Marshall once asked him not to refer to the navy as 'us' and to the army as 'them'.

Roosevelt was also the odd man out in another way; he was totally political. If you look at the others, you will see that they had other interests. All of them wrote books, though of different kinds. Roosevelt never wrote anything, except rather casual private letters. He did not even write his own speeches; he had an army of speech-writers labouring for him. However, some of the finest phrases, such as 'the only thing we have to fear is fear itself', were inserted by Roosevelt at the last moment.

His background did not prepare him at all to be a war lord. In theory, of course, he was a war lord from the moment he became president of the United States. Under the terms of the American constitution, the president is always the commander-in-chief of the armed forces.

But in 1933, when Roosevelt first became president, he was far from thinking in warlike terms. In those days, he had to save his country from a tremendous economic crisis, perhaps the worst

*The young Roosevelt at
L'Orient during First World
War*

crisis that any modern country has ever faced. It was the force of
his personality, his improvisations, his readiness to pursue any
kind of policy in order to restore confidence, which began the
New Deal and lifted the United States up from the Great Depression.

Roosevelt had no preconceived ideas about economics or, for
that matter, about war. I am tempted to say that he had no principles. I do not mean by that that he was wicked, but that he
operated only in response to a situation, and decided only at the
very last minute. There is a story from the early days of the New
Deal, when the dollar had gone off the gold standard and two
economists came to see him. One of them had a paper advising
that the dollar should go back on to the gold standard. The other
one had a paper advising quite the contrary—that it should be
allowed to float and to depreciate. Roosevelt looked through the
two papers and said: 'Take these into the next room and mix
them together.' This was always his reaction when faced with
contradictory arguments: 'Go away and mix them together.'

Averell Harriman said of him: People make a great mistake if,
when the president says 'yes', they think it means he agrees with

*President Franklin Delano Roosevelt*

them. It only means: 'Well, I've heard what you say, but I'm not going to make up my mind now.' Again and again, to people in the United States, to foreign statesmen, Roosevelt would say 'yes'. For instance, when Molotov came over from the Soviet Union to plead for a second front, Roosevelt said, 'Yes, there must be a second front this year,' but he only meant that this was how he felt at that moment; also he felt it was a useful thing to say to Molotov.

By his hesitations he allowed situations to develop. The basis of his policy was the eternal question-mark—what would the president do? It was only towards the end of the 1930s that he became

*Mrs Eleanor Roosevelt*

drawn into foreign affairs at all. Indeed, in his earlier years he was the most isolationist of all American presidents, convinced that it was America's duty to concentrate on her own recovery and still more on her own wealth.

As the situation in Europe and the Far East moved towards war, Roosevelt refused to be committed. He went on hoping that the menace of the eternal question-mark about America's policy would restrain the other countries from going to war. At the time of Munich, for instance, he refused to give the slightest commitment or suggestion of support to the British and the French. Even in 1939, although he expressed disapproval of Hitler's policy, he was careful not to commit himself to the British and the French. What did Roosevelt really intend to do? There are two conflicting answers. One, given by his enemies within the United States (and he had many), was that he was set on war; he wanted to drag the American people into war on the Allied side and, in a similar way, he was set on dragging them into war against Japan. Some historians have traced a whole series of conspiracies by which Roosevelt drew America into the war. In my opinion, they were mistaken in reaching this conclusion.

Some of Roosevelt's associates, and some more detached historians, have taken the view that he did not know what he was going to do.

For four months—from the fall of France in June 1940 to the end of the Battle of Britain in the following October—Roosevelt had doubts whether Britain would survive. But uppermost in his mind were not thoughts of going to the aid of Britain; his primary anxiety was to ensure that, in the event of Britain being invaded, the Royal Navy would be sent to the New World. Churchill

*Chicago soup kitchen during the Great Depression*

*Roosevelt watches launching of cargo Liberty ship*

133

*Boeing aircraft factory Seattle, 1942*

refused to promise this; he said that even to consider the plan would imply that we could consider defeat, and defeat was inconceivable.

From early 1941, Roosevelt's policy was simply to build up Great Britain's resources, to keep her going, to maintain her independence. Until when? Until what? Until America could come into the war? Or until both Great Britain and Germany wearied of war and would accept some sort of compromise? It is impossible to say.

Of course, what you have to bear in mind is that, despite being president, despite being re-elected not only in 1936, but again in 1940, and ultimately in 1944, Roosevelt was very restricted by American opinion. (Incidentally, he will always be unique in being American president four times; it had never happened before, and now, because of a constitutional amendment, it can never happen again.)

He was intensely apprehensive of public opinion, and, according to some good judges, often dragged behind it. He certainly did not wish to lead it until the situation was ripe. In 1940, for instance, it would have been difficult for Roosevelt, for the American government, to send economic aid to Great Britain. By the spring of 1941, the situation had changed: Americans were saying 'all aid short of war'. It was then that Roosevelt made his first great stroke—his 'lend-lease' plan for the supply of war materials to the Allies. This ensured that Great Britain, sustained by American aid, would stay in the war. Of course, there was another side to it. Thanks to lend-lease, the British and, later, the Russians, did the fighting and the Americans made the profit, at least for some time.

Though Roosevelt admired British courage and was anxious for British independence, he had a poor opinion of the British Empire. Curiously enough, he seems to have regarded Stalin's tyranny with a much gentler eye. In 1943, when he was in Teheran, he discussed the Indian problem with Stalin and said: 'Of course, Churchill's an old Tory; we can't trust him with India. The real answer, I think, will be to introduce the thorough Soviet system and make India anew.' Maybe this was merely the kind of thing he would say to Stalin. But he had a deep distrust of what he called British imperialism; he even talked at one time of handing Hong Kong over to China. He was deeply opposed to continuing

135

*Pearl Harbor, 1941*

the British Empire after the war was over; and even more hostile to the French Empire, particularly as it had been defeated.

Sometimes, reading Roosevelt's letters, you would think that he disliked de Gaulle even more than he disliked Hitler. To Roosevelt, de Gaulle represented an arrogant independence. The very fact that de Gaulle had nothing meant that he could behave in an independent way; Churchill, on the other hand, had to be more co-operative.

There was a considerable element of personal friendship between Churchill and Roosevelt, but then, with Roosevelt, there was always personal friendship when he needed it. He was entirely a man who lived for giving himself out; he was one of those men who, when he was alone in a room, you felt he was not there at all. He had to have company, but his conversation was always on the surface; he never said anything profound, he never expressed profound views, even about the war. To him, apparently, the war was entirely caused by a shortage of raw materials for some of the powers, and he often said that one of the ways of preventing or ending the war would be to agree on sharing out equally the raw materials of the world. America was for him the privileged country. For instance, when lend-lease came into being, part of the bargain was that the British must cut down their exports, must become totally economically dependent on the United States. As Keynes said of the British: 'We threw good housekeeping to the wind, but we saved the world.' Although the Americans supplied the weapons of war, they also squeezed Great Britain dry economically; and that was Roosevelt's deliberate policy.

*American Congress votes for declaration of war, 1941*

*MacKenzie King, Roosevelt and Churchill at Quebec, 1943*

Did he lure Japan and the American people into war? I am confident he did not. He made mistakes. He imposed an economic embargo on Japan, which, inevitably, was a delayed declaration of war. But the actual attack on Pearl Harbor was a total surprise; it was not foreseen by Roosevelt. Indeed, I will tell you briefly why the surprise was so complete.

For about a fortnight before the attack on Pearl Harbor, the Japanese navy had maintained radio silence. It is nonsense to say that there was ever a series of radio messages which the Americans could have broken. What they knew was that Japan was going to war somewhere. At the very last moment, when the Japanese sent an ultimatum to the Americans, an American code officer deduced that Pearl Harbor would be attacked, because one o'clock, the time when the message would be delivered in Washington, was sunrise at Pearl Harbor. He told his chief, Admiral Stark, of his fears. Stark said: 'But the defence of Pearl Harbor is a matter for the army.' So the matter was passed over to General Marshall the army chief. Marshall was out riding. When he got back and saw the message he said: 'Oh, we must send a warning, mustn't we, that they're going to be attacked in an hour's time.' He then discovered that the army's signals had been stood down for the day. There was no question of asking the navy to send the message: 'I'm not going to ask the navy to send it; that would be too degrading,' he said. So he sent the message by commercial lines. They, however, stopped at San Francisco, resulting in the telegram being held up for a quarter of an hour. Finally, it arrived at the telegraph office at Pearl Harbor. It was

*Roosevelt and his advisers at Yalta, 1945*

*Admiral E. J. King, Naval
Chief of Staff*

*Admiral C. W. Nimitz,
Commander-in-Chief of the
Pacific Fleet*

140

*American Aircraft Carrier, Pacific Fleet*

given to a messenger, who, incidentally, was a Japanese, to take up to command headquarters. He got on his bicycle and was loyally pedalling away when the bombs began to fall.

Pearl Harbor solved Roosevelt's problem, for he would have had great difficulty in bringing the American people into the war if it had not been for the Japanese attack on it and the German ultimatum that followed.

From that time, from December 1941 onwards, Roosevelt was commander-in-chief of the American armed forces in practice as well as in theory. He exercised command in a very different way from either Stalin or Churchill. He certainly did not control all the distant armies. He did not even sit in with the chiefs of staff to any great extent; in fact, Roosevelt never liked formal meetings. What he liked was sitting around late at night with one or two old friends, people he could rely on, trying out this idea and that, and then arriving at decisions. This approach to presidential decision-making was something which often disturbed Churchill, and disturbed the even tenor of negotiations between the British and American chiefs of staff. Suddenly, without previous warning, without explaining why it had been made, the president would announce a decision. One American military historian has calculated that there were 22 different occasions, all of great importance, when Roosevelt, without explanation, overrode all his professional advisers.

The first decision he made at the start of the war, one that was to shape its course for two years, was a decision which was in accordance with his professional advisers: to put the war in Europe first. It is an amazing thing, considering what happened at Pearl Harbor, that the American people did not insist on dealing with Japan first. But Roosevelt argued very simply: 'Germany is the greater enemy; once we've defeated Germany, we shall be able to deal with Japan.'

*Roosevelt inspects U.S. troops at Casablanca*

*Planning the invasion: Tedder, Eisenhower and Montgomery, February 1944*

There followed from this decision something which was his initiative much more. General Marshall, the American generals, the General Staff, wanted to prepare a single thing: a vast build-up of arms, and then an invasion of northern Europe. The British were already fighting in North Africa, and Churchill wanted the African war to be extended. Roosevelt at first indicated approval of what his military advisers were doing, and then, quite suddenly, came down on the other side. He accepted the British argument that you could not have an invasion of northern Europe in 1942, and said: 'If we can't invade northern Europe, we must go somewhere else, and that somewhere else is not the Pacific.'

The decisive voice in putting the American weight into the Mediterranean campaign, first in North Africa and then in Italy, and in postponing the second front in northern Europe until 1944, was Roosevelt's, And why do you think he made it initially? Because the congressional elections were coming up in November 1942, and he wanted American soldiers to be actually engaged in

143

*Cautious Eisenhower and impulsive Patton, 1945*

144

*General Stilwell*

battle before that time; it would be a good way of swinging the vote. Ironically, the soldiers were delayed and did not arrive in North Africa until a week after the elections; but by then the momentum had been given.

Roosevelt did much more in determining the character of the war. He was more concerned about keeping in step with the British than the American generals were, and to sustain Churchill and the British spirit in the European field. He never had the slightest interest in the British war in the Far East; he regarded it as an embarrassment that they should be there at all. But he needed the British as a loyal second. And he had the strangest and simplest ideas of how the world should be run after the war. Until quite late in the day, his solution to all postwar problems was that every country in the world except the United States would be disarmed, and that the United States would be the world policeman. Then, on reflection, he decided that the British could be cut in, too; they would be allowed to maintain a rather smaller army than the Americans and they would be policemen

*U.S. troops land at Salerno, 1943*

along with them. I am sure, though, that the British would not have been allowed to police their own empire. At a later stage still, when the Russians were in fact doing more fighting than the British and Americans combined, Roosevelt recognised that his plan would not work; the Soviet Union would maintain her great army whether he approved of it or not. After that, the whole idea faded away. But it was an idea which was characteristic of him, something that he had thought of late at night: 'I've got it. Let the Americans run the world—that'll provide peace and prosperity for everybody.'

Of course, he also thought that all countries should have exactly the same outlook as the Americans, the American democratic system and, most of all, the American economic system—what has been well called not so much free trade as free investment; that if the American capitalists were allowed to invest all over the world without any restrictions, then this would produce a prosperous world. It would certainly have produced prosperity for the Americans. But Roosevelt was also a man of great ideals. He was the only war lord who really believed that the United Nations was the essential way forward for mankind, and that it would work.

Regarding war, he again took a simple, though in this sense a wise, view: that the way to win a modern war was to have far more of everything than your opponents. When the Americans came to fight their battles in northern Europe against the Germans, they did not achieve much by superior strategy, though they achieved something by surprise. But what they basically achieved was simply to win by weight. As one American put it: 'For America, war meant a mass-production war. You design something on the production line, you lay it on and there it is.' By 1944, Great Britain had become much overshadowed by this American power, which Roosevelt had developed by always setting the targets higher than any American industrialist thought would be poss-

*U.S. troops on their way to Bologna, 1944*

*U.S. tanks and battered Italian town, 1944*

*Chiang Kai-Shek, Roosevelt and Churchill at Cairo, 1943*

ible, and these being achieved.

Roosevelt's greatest political stroke, in his opinion, was to establish good relations with Stalin. When Churchill met Stalin, they sometimes rowed, they sometimes agreed, but they discussed serious problems in detail. When Roosevelt met Stalin, he was confident that his skill in dealing with people would win Stalin over. His main stroke was not to say to Stalin: 'Well, I recognise the frontiers of 1941' (which he refused to do), but to tell Stalin: 'You know, Churchill and I call you Uncle Joe in private.' Stalin, far from being amused, was extremely offended and asked: 'Is that a Western idea of a joke?' I think it was a joke, but I do not think it was one that Stalin ever learned to appreciate.

Stalin must have found this strange, evasive man with his back-slapping manner, his easygoing talk, a very mysterious person to deal with. On the other hand, Roosevelt, unlike most Americans, did not regard the Russians as totally divided from them by a barrier of principle. On the contrary, he was the one statesman in Great Britain or in America or in any west Euro-

*U.S. Marines on Bougainville Island, 1945*

*U.S. troops in Aachen, 1944*

pean country, the one Western statesman who not only tried to get on really intimate terms with the Soviet Union, but believed that he could do it, and largely did so. Relations between West and East were warmer in Roosevelt's time, not because, as people say, he made unreasonable concessions, but because he was the only Western statesman of that period who really treated the Soviet Union as an equal. And towards the end of his life, he was more concerned to be on close terms with the Soviet Union than he was with Great Britain, simply because the Russians had power. How the situation would have developed after the war was over is something we shall never know. Roosevelt did not have much detailed knowledge about overseas countries. For instance, at all the discussions about Germany and the future of Germany, he would say: 'Well, I know Germany very well; I went on a bicycle tour there when I was a boy.' And so Roosevelt had to be the authority on Germany because he had once bicycled there.

When the frontiers of Poland were discussed, Roosevelt was

*U.S. landing craft at Leyte*

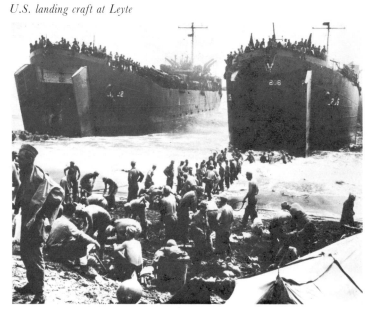

*Churchill, Roosevelt and Stalin at Yalta*

*U.S. landing craft at Okinawa*

quite ready to give a great deal of Polish territory to the Soviet
Union. But he also remembered there was a town called Lwow,
which he had once read about in a geography book, so he kept
saying to Stalin: 'Well, do you think Lwow could stay in Poland?'
Stalin must have been absolutely bewildered by this. What he
may have understood better was Roosevelt's explanation of what
represented to him the real crux of the Polish problem: 'You see
there are a lot of Polish voters in the United States and, very
shortly, there'll be an election to make me president again, so I
must be soft with the Poles.'

This strange man, the most enigmatic of the war lords, though perhaps not the greatest of them, was the most successful; it was Roosevelt who made the United States the most powerful country in the world. But now, if one looks at him again, there is a sort of emptiness about him.

He died before the end of the war, although victory was in sight; and his achievements, limited or otherwise, were repudiated, brushed aside. Incidentally, one of the things he did, or rather did not do, greatly affected the British position after the war. In 1942, Great Britain gave all her nuclear secrets to America. Roosevelt, in his casual way, made a personal promise that, after the war was over, Great Britain should be allowed to share America's scientific secrets. The promise was not passed on to Roosevelt's successor, and was not kept. Again and again, you feel that Roosevelt operated from day to day. After saying, for instance, that he meant American troops to run the whole world, he said to Stalin at Yalta in 1945: 'We shall be pulling out our troops in two years' time; you and the British will have to run it.' But nevertheless he had this enormous capacity for accepting responsibility. He was undoubtedly the boss.

There is a strange story about his private life. In 1913, he had fallen in love with his wife's social secretary. He wished to have a divorce and marry the girl, but his family insisted that this would ruin his political career. He acquiesced, and the two parted. Eleanor Roosevelt never shared a bedroom with her husband again. In the meantime, the girl married. Almost 30 years later, and after she had become a widow, she and Roosevelt met again and renewed their love. It was all kept intensely secret. The powerful American Secret Service provided all its resources to ensure that the President could be alleged to be going to one place when, in fact, he was meeting his friend in another. On many occasions, for instance, he would depart in a special train for some objective, say down in Georgia, and then it would be switched into a siding, where another special train would draw up beside it, and the two would be able to spend a couple of days together. Occasionally, when Eleanor Roosevelt was in Europe or somewhere like that, the Secret Service would smuggle Roosevelt's friend into the White House.

As his physique declined, Roosevelt spent more and more time in the country near the lady's house, so that she could come over

*Roosevelt; the funeral*

and visit him every day. In his last weeks, he was there all the time; in fact, for a fortnight or so, the United States was being run, or its policy was being determined, not by the president but by General Marshall, the chief of staff.

One morning in April 1945, Roosevelt suddenly said to the lady: 'I've got a dreadful headache.' He then fell unconscious. Before a doctor was summoned, the Secret Service snatched up the lady, put her in a car and whisked her away from the scene. She never saw Roosevelt again.

Later, when Mrs Roosevelt learnt of this story, she was indignant. Roosevelt's daughter said: 'But Mother, Father was a very lonely man.'

# 6

## *WAR LORDS ANONYMOUS*

---

# War Lords Anonymous

The Japanese have some claim, I suppose, to the original war lords. Their country, for some hundreds of years, was under the control of war lords—the samurai. And yet, in the Second World War, the Japanese diverged entirely from the pattern which I have been presenting in previous lectures: there was no Japanese war lord—no single figure who led Japan into war, who directed the war, who made the decisions, and so on.

It is often supposed that General Tojo was such a war lord. It is true that, for quite a long time, he had been a leading general in the war with China. It is also true that he was minister of war before the Second World War and indeed became prime minister just before it started. Ironically, he was made prime minster in the hope that he would keep the army under control, and maybe that Japan would not go to war after all. He ceased to be prime minister before the war ended, and played no role in ending the war. He was simply representative of a wide class of generals, of admirals and, to some extent, of civilians, who contributed towards making policy or allowing the policy of Japan to happen.

Until 1867 or thereabouts, Japan had not existed as a power, but had lain open, a victim, supposedly, to the penetration and to the imperialism of the European powers and the United States. But when Japan was forcibly opened by American gunboats, the Japanese, by an extraordinary effort of decision, determined they would make themselves into Europeans. The traditional system was overthrown, and the emperor, or mikado, who had merely

*Admiral Togo, victor of the Battle of Tsushima*

been a religious figure for hundreds of years, was suddenly brought out and made the figurehead of what is known as the Meiji revolution.

Then, within 20 years, Japan learned all the lessons of Europe: it learned about constitutionalism and established a parliament; it learned about industrialism; it learned about modern armies; it learned about navies. But in its learning there was what one might call a rigidity. What the Japanese were doing was not something that had grown out of their history. The other men I have been talking about—even Hitler, for instance—grew out of their countries' history and cannot be properly understood without understanding the history. Modern Japan grew out of European history, and the Japanese view was that if they loyally, carefully, pedantically followed the European patterns, they would be

159

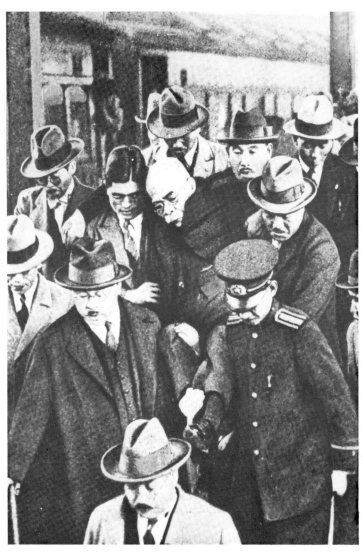

*Attempted assassination of Prime Minister Yoko Hamaguchi, 1930*

transformed into an acceptable member of the great power family. In some ways, they were.

Certainly, Japan became one of the great industrial powers of the world. It also developed a great navy, developed it to the extent that, particularly after the First World War, there were only three recognised naval powers in the world—the United States, Great Britain and Japan. Japan also had a great army.

As early as 1904, the Japanese showed they were capable of war. Although greatly inferior in strength to Russia, both on land and sea, they defeated Russia in the Russo-Japanese war of 1904 to 1905, achieving the greatest naval victory since Trafalgar, at the battle of Tsushima. It is often thought that the Japanese navy was stronger than the Russian. In fact, it was inferior, the relationship being ten to four. Admiral Togo, the commander-in-chief of the Japanese navy, won by superior ingenuity.

Japan joined the Allies during the First World War and was thus one of the victorious powers which attended the peace conference in Paris. At this, there was one very significant incident; one which illustrated that the Japanese had been cheated. They had been told that, if they followed the European model, they would be accepted as a civilised power. Therefore, when they proposed a clause laying down racial equality, they assumed it would be accepted.

It was defeated by none other than President Wilson, the idealist who preached the League of Nations and all the other things of the New World. The Japanese realised that this was a fraud: at the very time when they were supposedly being treated as equals, a total ban was being placed on the migration of Japanese into the United States. Other nationalities were let in more freely. The Japanese learnt a lesson: the rules which applied to white men did not apply to what Churchill used to call 'those funny little yellow folk'. Racial equality was far from being achieved. This, among other things, no doubt made the Japanese more sensitive and more aggressive.

In the hierarchy of order in Japan, every decision came from the emperor; his power was absolute, at least in theory. The 19th-century Japanese revolutionaries who made this rule about the emperor's power as part of the constitution had soon realised that if, in fact, every decision came from the emperor, he would make bad ones as well as good ones, and would be discredited. It was therefore laid down that no course of action should ever be submitted to the emperor until there was total agreement among the ministers and among the armed forces. Therefore, faced with a unanimous resolution, the emperor never had anything to do except agree. We know how an imperial council was held. Ministers, generals and admirals filed in. They then stood up throughout the meeting, with the emperor sitting a little aloof, listening to them, nodding his head. They made their speeches, making it clear that they all agreed. The emperor then would say: 'I agree.' That was the extent of his power. Because what was put to him had already been settled, he was never able to say: 'I don't agree.'

*Japanese troops in Shanghai, 1932*

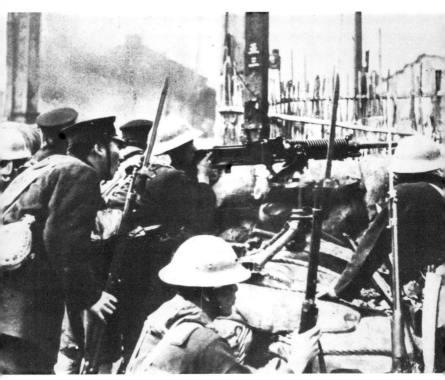

Although we talk about a Japanese ministry and a Japanese prime minister, the functions of these bore little resemblance to what existed in constitutional countries such as Great Britain. The civilian ministers ran civil affairs and that only. Military affairs—not only how the army was organised, but actual military decisions—rested entirely with the army general staff. Naval decisions rested entirely with the naval general staff. And, once war had started, there was a convention, decisive in Japanese history and policy, called 'the autonomy of the supreme command'. Wherever there was war—against Russia in 1904 to 1905, against China in the 1930s—the supreme command was autonomous,

*Japanese Marines in Shanghai, 1932*

*Japanese soldiers make obeissance towards Emperor*

once conflict had started. Nobody could tell it what to do; the war had to be left to the man in the field.

In every ministry, it was essential that there should be an army minister and a navy minister. Indeed, if either of them resigned, the ministry was automatically dissolved. The army minister was nominated by the army staff, and the navy minister was nominated by the navy staff. Either of those staffs could wreck a ministry by pulling out their minister. In the 1920s, Japan looked as if it were moving towards a liberal system, but in the 1930s, during political changes and during the war with China, the two armed services counted for more and more and, in a negative way, could dictate to a ministry. Of course, the ministry could also dictate to them, because it could say: 'No, we won't follow your policy.' This meant that no ministry could be formed but it also meant that there would be no army minister, no navy minister.

The army minister and the navy minister themselves possessed no army or naval power. They were the agents of their respective staffs. If the navy minister wanted one thing and the navy staff wanted another, he had to conform. The civilian ministers followed one policy of diplomacy and alliances, the army another, the navy another.

Until quite late in the day, there was no co-operation between navy and army. It was only in 1937 that an institution was set up called a liaison conference, at which the chiefs of the army and navy staff met and discussed things, though they very often did not agree. For most of the time, the army wanted a war against Russia because that meant a lot of fighting on land. The navy wanted a war against the United States or Great Britain because that meant fighting at sea. You could also add that the civilian ministers did not particularly want war either on land or at sea, but wanted the gains of war. All of them wanted Japan to be a

*Admiral Yamamoto, the planner of Pearl Harbor*

great power.

A force in Japan, one unique to it, was a passionate patriotism among the younger officers. There were also many younger men in civilian life who believed that there was not sufficient patriotism in Japan. And so it came about that in Japan, as in no other country, assassination became an ordinary political weapon. Unlike the organised party violence you got with the Nazis, the assassinations in Japan were the work of individuals. These individuals had been told it was their duty to serve the nation and that if a minister, or for that matter a general, was not serving the nation adequately, then it was right to assassinate him. In a short space of time, two prime ministers were assas-

*Emperor Hirohito inspects the bomb damage in Tokyo*

*Emperor Hirohito in priest's robes and with priest's sceptre*

sinated, one after the other, also a number of generals and leading officers. From then on, all those who followed a cautious, sane policy did so with great stealth. If they appeared to be too cautious, they would be certain to be assassinated. Not that the Japanese ministers and officers feared assassination in itself; it was that their assassination made their policies ineffective. Therefore, far from the leaders conspiring to bring about war, as often happens in history, they conspired to bring about peace or, at any rate, to slow things down.

The mainspring of Japanese policy came from the Great Depression. The Japanese had loyally accepted a world system of free trade. They had become capitalists, like others, because they thought that by doing this they would enter the magic circle. But during the Depression the world began to close against them. The United States had enormous tariff barriers. The British Empire put up tariff barriers under the name of Protection. Japan was squeezed in and, unlike Britain and the United States, did not have overseas interests. The United States claimed not just the

*General Tojo, Japanese Prime Minister at outbreak of war*

*Japanese anti-aircraft gunners, 1939*

United States but most of the American continent as an American sphere of influence. In the 1930s, all the South American states were economic dependants of the United States and were a protected market for American goods. The British Empire, which extended across the world, was a protected market for British goods. The Japanese for their part tended to take the view that the Far East was their sphere. Most of this sphere was in China, and China was in a weak, disorganised state. In September 1931, the Japanese encouraged Manchuria to declare its independence from China and in 1932 set it up as a puppet state under the name of Manchukuo. Fundamentally, what the Japanese were saying was that, just as the British were entitled to control their empire,

169

*Japanese landing in Hong Kong, 1941*

*British prisoners of war at Singapore, 1942*

most of which, incidentally, was not British but was inhabited by coloured people such as Indians and Africans, just as the Americans were entitled to control most of the American continent, so too were the Japanese entitled to control the area of Asia which was not inhabited by Europeans at all. And you must remember, when thinking how scandalous it was that the Japanese should try to interfere in Chinese internal affairs so as to impose order for the maintenance of their trade, that an example had been set them by others. In 1860, for instance, the British and the French, after Chinese interference with British trade, marched on Peking and destroyed and looted the summer palace.

Throughout the 1930s, the Japanese, increasingly thwarted by Chinese opposition, pressed into Chinese territory by military means. Not yet did they encounter the effective opposition of either the United States or Britain, though these countries made

*Japanese warships burning at Battle of Midway Island*

*Japanese troops salute the Rising Sun*

constant protests and rebukes. But neither got the message over. The Americans stood by their open door policy—that China, just like every other part of the world except the United States, should be wide open to everybody's trade. From behind their own tariff wall, the Americans wanted to trade all over the world, to have no barriers erected against them. The Japanese answered with the argument of respective spheres.

As the shadows of war, and then the realities of war itself, spread more and more across the world—when Germany went to war with Great Britain and France, when France fell—both the United States and Japan were desperately anxious to gain supremacy over the other, to get their own way. It was a classic example of each side believing that it could get its own way without war. The Japanese said: 'If we increase the tension, the Americans will give way because they are so worried about the

*Japanese artillery on the Burma front*

*Japanese troops attack in Burma*

British in Europe.' The Americans, on the other hand, said: 'If we increase the tension, the Japanese will crumble because they are the weaker.'

The decisive step towards war was taken not by the Japanese but by President Roosevelt when in 1941 he placed a total embargo on oil supplies to Japan. Japan had no oil of its own, and got most of it from the Dutch East Indies and a little from other places. Once this embargo had been placed, it was clear to the Japanese that, within not more than 18 months, Japanese oil would run out and Japan would collapse as a great power. This is exactly what Roosevelt foresaw, and he believed that the threat of

*Japanese tanks on the advance in Burma*

this happening would make the Japanese accept his terms. These were that the Japanese would withdraw all their forces from China; would renounce any position of being a great power; and would accept the Americans' open door policy, which would make the United States the dominant economic force throughout the Chinese mainland.

The Japanese had no illusions that they were stronger than the Americans, but as they contemplated the world situation in the autumn of 1941, it was inevitable that they were tempted to defy the Americans. They were tempted, because all Japan's former opponents, except the United States, now seemed defenceless. France had collapsed, Holland had been overrun, and as far as Britain was concerned, it was clear that it already had too much to do in Europe to be able to hold on to its position in Singapore. At least, it was clear to everyone except a few people in London, who had a fantasy that Singapore was a strongly occupied base.

Therefore, if the Japanese simply went into South East Asia (and that was their vision of the war), they would, with very little difficulty, create a great empire. But in the Pacific, at Pearl Har-

*Japanese light tank*

*British patrol in Bahe, Burma*

*Japanese bicycle unit on advance in Burma*

bor, the United States had a great naval base. From there, the United States could threaten the Japanese flank and take action which would lead to a crumbling of this empire.

There were, in fact, two quite different spheres of war. One was South East Asia, an area which the Japanese wished to move into and exploit; the other was what came to be called the Pacific war, in which all the Japanese wanted was that the Americans should be pushed back.

The solution to the problem of Pearl Harbor was found by one of the few geniuses which the Second World War produced, Admiral Yamamoto: that Pearl Harbor and its fleet should be eliminated. He put forward his plan at a meeting at which was being discussed whether or not to go to war. When the emperor was urged by his advisers to approve the declaration of war, it

*Japanese tank trap: soldier and bomb set to explode together*

was the one occasion when he actually said something. He pulled out of his pocket a poem and read it:

> All the seas in every quarter
> Are as brothers to one another.
> Why, then, do the winds and waves of strife
> Rage so turbulently throughout the world?

'That,' he said, 'is a poem which I often have in mind.' And that was the only attempt that he made to contribute to policy. The decison taken was that, unless the United States dropped their opposition, Japan would go to war.

It is often said that the Americans ought to have known that Pearl Harbor was going to be attacked; but the Japanese themselves, apart from those who planned the attack, did not know—even the navy general staff in Tokyo was not sure. All it knew was that the Japanese navy was going to attack somewhere.

Pearl Harbor certainly began the Second World War, from the Japanese point of view. And, although in his surprise attack on Pearl Harbor he had achieved one of the greatest strategical strokes of the Second World War, Admiral Yamamoto said: 'I fear we have only awakened a sleeping giant, and his reaction will be terrible.' And so it proved.

The Japanese attacked Pearl Harbor and did much serious damage to its warships and naval and military installations, and they overran the whole of South East Asia; but they never imagined they could penetrate to the New World and invade the United States. They did not even imagine that, if there were a prolonged war between them and the United States, they would win it. What they hoped for was that the United States, mainly involved in the European war, with so much of its resources directed towards Europe, would weary and would, in the end, come to a compromise with Japan.

From April 1942, when the Japanese had, on the one side, extended to Burma and, on the other side, almost to Australia, they were fighting a defensive war, hoping to wear the other side

*The 'Little Boy' nuclear bomb as detonated over Hiroshima, August 1945*

*Hiroshima 1945*

down. They had no direction; they had administration. There was no really single outstanding Japanese general.

There were a number of decisive naval battles, for whoever controlled the Pacific could maintain the political and strategic position. Yamamoto attempted to do, at the battle of Midway in June 1942, what he had done at Pearl Harbor or, rather, to complete his action there. Instead, in a few minutes, with the use of aircraft launched from aircraft carriers, the Americans reversed the situation and from that time onwards the enormous Japanese

*Nuclear cloud over Nagasaki, August 1945*

*The Japanese surrender to MacArthur, 2nd September 1945*

navy was increasingly on the defensive in its turn.

The Japanese owed their ultimate defeat to two things. One was the incredible economic strength of the United States, which enabled it, by 1943, to conduct both the war in Europe and the war in the Pacific. Against all Japanese calculations, the Americans were clearing up both at the same time. The other thing which led to Japan's defeat was its terrible mistake of neglecting to provide itself with anti-submarine devices. By 1943, Japan's mercantile marine had lost three-quarters of its strength. Now remember, Japan, even more than Great Britain, depended for everything on supplies from overseas. By 1944, it was almost impossible for them to supply even their essential naval and military bases. In this way, blockade was probably as decisive as the more dramatic military and naval engagements.

By the beginning of 1945, most of the Japanese civilians and some of the more cautious generals recognised that the war was lost. From then on, just as they had spent six months thinking about going to war, the Japanese reflected on how they could get out of it. And yet, none of the ministers or generals or admirals dared to speak about defeat openly, because of the shadow of assassination or military rebellion which still hung over them. Even when negotiations were started, they had to be conducted in great secrecy. The generals did not rule, nor did the admirals; it was the anonymous assassin who, it seemed, might really determine policy.

By August 1945, the American navy said firmly that Japan would collapse simply because her seaborne trade was at an end. But the American air force was anxious to use the nuclear weapon. The American army, in its turn, talked of an eventual

*Japanese surrender at Singapore, 12th September 1945*

*Emperor Hirohito visits General MacArthur*

million army casualties in the war. In the end, the nuclear bomb was used against Japan, not so much as the result of any serious calculation, but simply because the Americans felt that, as they had the bomb, they had better use it.

After the bomb was dropped on Hiroshima, the Japanese emperor intervened and insisted that peace should be made. He said: 'We have resolved to endure the unendurable and suffer what is insufferable.' The decision to surrender unconditionally had already been made before the second bomb was dropped on Nagasaki.

On 2 September 1945, General MacArthur formally accepted the unconditional surrender of Japan. One of his aides asked him: 'Are you going to call on the emperor?' MacArthur replied: 'No, the emperor will come to me.' And sure enough, a few days later, Emperor Hirohito did. He said: 'I come to you, General Mac-Arthur, to offer myself to the judgement of the powers you represent as the one who bears sole responsibility for every political and military decison made and action taken by my people in the conduct of the war.' He was not charged as a war criminal, and there was no reason why he should have been. But others, including General Tojo, were charged, tried and sentenced to death.

But the Japanese learnt the lesson of the Second World War more than anyone else has done. Japan is the only great power which has steadfastly refused to make or to possess nuclear weapons. In this the Japanese set an example to us all.

# Index

# READ MORE IN PENGUIN

In every corner of the world, on every subject under the sun, Penguin represents quality and variety – the very best in publishing today.

For complete information about books available from Penguin – including Puffins, Penguin Classics and Arkana – and how to order them, write to us at the appropriate address below. Please note that for copyright reasons the selection of books varies from country to country.

**In the United Kingdom**: Please write to *Dept. JC, Penguin Books Ltd, FREEPOST, West Drayton, Middlesex UB7 OBR.*

If you have any difficulty in obtaining a title, please send your order with the correct money, plus ten per cent for postage and packaging, to *PO Box No. 11, West Drayton, Middlesex UB7 OBR*

**In the United States**: Please write to *Consumer Sales, Penguin USA, P.O. Box 999, Dept. 17109, Bergenfield, New Jersey 07621-0120.* VISA and MasterCard holders call 1-800-253-6476 to order all Penguin titles

**In Canada**: Please write to *Penguin Books Canada Ltd, 10 Alcorn Avenue, Suite 300, Toronto, Ontario M4V 3B2*

**In Australia**: Please write to *Penguin Books Australia Ltd, P.O. Box 257, Ringwood, Victoria 3134*

**In New Zealand**: Please write to *Penguin Books (NZ) Ltd, Private Bag 102902, North Shore Mail Centre, Auckland 10*

**In India**: Please write to *Penguin Books India Pvt Ltd, 706 Eros Apartments, 56 Nehru Place, New Delhi 110 019*

**In the Netherlands**: Please write to *Penguin Books Netherlands bv, Postbus 3507, NL-1001 AH Amsterdam*

**In Germany**: Please write to *Penguin Books Deutschland GmbH, Metzlerstrasse 26, 60594 Frankfurt am Main*

**In Spain**: Please write to *Penguin Books S. A., Bravo Murillo 19, 1° B, 28015 Madrid*

**In Italy**: Please write to *Penguin Italia s.r.l., Via Felice Casati 20, I–20124 Milano*

**In France**: Please write to *Penguin France S. A., 17 rue Lejeune, F–31000 Toulouse*

**In Japan**: Please write to *Penguin Books Japan, Ishikiribashi Building, 2–5–4, Suido, Bunkyo-ku, Tokyo 112*

**In Greece**: Please write to *Penguin Hellas Ltd, Dimocritou 3, GR–106 71 Athens*

**In South Africa**: Please write to *Longman Penguin Southern Africa (Pty) Ltd, Private Bag X08, Bertsham 2013*